Karl-Heinz Becker | Michael Dörner

Cooking Recipes for Fractals
Computer graphics experiments with Python

Cooking Recipes for Fractals

Computer Graphics Experiments with Python

Karl-Heinz Becker | Michael Dörfler

IT:compact

---

[1]   Teacher and scientist Karl-Heinz Becker and Michael Dörfler
work as IT lecturers ...

The world of reality has
its limits, the world of imagination is limitless.

– Jean-Jacques Rousseau

Contents

1 Foreword

Cooking as an activity is known to be one of the oldest cultural techniques of mankind. However, this book is not about edible things for which there are recipes. The activity of programming can also be considered a cultural technique. For programming, there are cooking recipes in programming languages as practical examples for many standard tasks.

Our cooking recipes listed here create visual meals. These are computer graphics that look beautiful and elegant. You can hang such graphics on your wall or send them in postcard size for different occasions. These are certainly special cards that are guaranteed to generate interesting enquiries from the recipients. So if you want to produce fancy, beautiful images for blank walls, greeting cards or more spectacular other artefacts (3D printing, cutting plotters, etc.), you have found the right subject of fractal computer graphics here.

Unlike the three basic books (Volumes 1, 2, 3 - see note on page 137) - you will not find any fundamental derivations here, neither concerning the underlying mathematics, nor concerning the programming language Python. [1]Mathematically, we have picked out a nice special case of fractal objects. And programming-wise, we will provide them with a well-functioning construction kit of short code snippets to work with.

---

[1] Volume 1: Fractals and Dynamical Systems
Volume 2: Fractals XXL - Picture book of fractals
Volume 3: Newton Fractals
For more information, please see the appendix.

Deeper consideration and discussion of alternative approaches will not take place. Therefore, we call the offer *recipes*.

Recipes are known to be short but functional descriptions of steps that lead to success. Let's look at a cooking recipe for comparison, for example potato gratin. It begins with the beautiful sentence:

500 g potatoes, mainly waxy

What is not explained here are the complete basics, i.e. what a potato is, when it became native to Europe, what varieties there are, how it is planted, looked after, harvested, stored. Which ideological, nutritional and health-promoting questions follow here - all this is left out, it is just a *RECIPE*.

As soon as you have mastered the basic recipe, it is of course also permitted to make small(!) changes. We also want to expressly encourage you to do so. We are convinced that your experiments will lead to first successes and further developments.

Not only that, but we have chosen the programming language *Python* because this language offers many interesting additional libraries that facilitate visualization, i.e. the production of computer graphics.

Have fun with your cooking, experiments with computer graphics and learning an interesting programming language. Enjoy it!

Bremen, Karl-Heinz Becker / Michael Dörfler

Acknowledgements
The book was typeset with a LaTeX template using the eML template. The use of the LaTeX template is free according to CC0 1.0 Universal (CC0 1.0) Public Domain Dedication. Many thanks to Martin Wilhelm Leidig, member of Dante, the German-speaking association TeX e.V. Martin Leidig has developed the eML template (**e**ssential **M**ake it with **L**atex Template) with which this book is published. [2]

---

[2] The eML template is a further development of the Orange Book Template

2 Fundamentals of iterative fractals

The term *fractal* was defined in 1975 by Benoit Mandelbrot , who used it to characterize a whole class of forms, structures and patterns of the real and mathematical world. A class of real-world systems that can be modelled and described by differential equations is called *Dynamic Systems*. For example, dynamical systems that can be described by a mathematical model of a time-dependent process produce fractal structures called *strange attractors*.

Info   Fractal ▷ https://bit.ly/3Rpvb6H

There is a famous dynamic system called the Lorenz system, which is linked to a real world system, weather forecasting, and with an interesting history.

Info   E.Lorenz Chaos Attractor ▷ https://bit.ly/10UoL7H

Edward Lorenz's system of differential equations contains three numerical parameters that define and describe the state of the model atmosphere at a certain time.

Since this is a spatial model, we base it on an x, y, z coordinate system. The calculation and prediction of the behaviour of the system is done by inputting initial values, and the calculated values are fed back into the mathematical system of equations as new input values. Similar input values should produce similar final values. The opposite can be the case. Minimal changes in the initial values produced surprisingly different final values. This parameter-sensitive behaviour of the dynamical system defined by the Lorenz equations marked the birth of *chaos theory*, the state behaviour that can be described by *strange attractors*. This led to the realization that such graphical visualizations have fractal properties.

Info   Strange Attractor ▷ `https://bit.ly/3yuPKpR`

The Lorenz system, a family of three non-linear, coupled ordinary differential equations, with parameters a, b, c can be described by the following iteration equations:

$$\frac{dx}{dt} = x' = a \cdot (y - x)$$
$$\frac{dy}{dt} = y' = x \cdot (b - z) - y = x \cdot b - x \cdot z - y$$
$$\frac{dz}{dt} = z' = x \cdot y - c \cdot z$$

With this equation structure (using the Lorenz formulas as an example) we can program a method (subroutine) that displays the respective attractor in the different planes (xy, xz, yz as well as xyz(3d)) as a graph. We want to solve such and many other differential equations with numerical methods and draw the results ourselves.

Systems of differential equations can be solved elegantly with libraries of the Python programming language. The libraries - *numpy* - *scipy* - *matplotlib* are used. A visualization of the chaotic behaviour of a dynamical system described by these mathematical equations is done by default with the plot commands of the library *matplotlib*.

NumPy is a program library for the Python programming language that allows, for example, easy handling of multidimensional arrays. *SciPy* is a Python-based open source software environment. It is used by scientists, analysts and engineers for scientific computing, visualization and all related calculations, especially the numerical solution of differential equations. *Matplotlib* is a Python program library with which mathematical visualizations of all kinds can be created. We will need all three of these libraries for our recipes.

For the Lorenz attractor or its differential equation system, the programming (using the three libraries and their subroutines) and the visualization look like this:

```
1   import math
2   import numpy as np
3   import matplotlib. pyplot as plt
4   from mpl_toolkits. mplot3d import Axes3D
5   from scipy.integrate  import odeint

7   # Parameter
8   picname = "Lorenz_Standard"
9   a = 10
10  b = 28 # 28, 99.65, 100.5, 160, 350
11  c = 8.0/3.0
12  # basic equation
13  def calculate (u, t, a, b, c):
14      x, y, z = u
15      # Lorenz_Standard
16      dxdt = a*(y-x)
17      dydt = x*(b-z) - y
18      dzdt = x*y - c*z
19      return(dxdt, dydt, dzdt)

21  # start values and initialization
22  y0 = 0.1,  0.1,  0.1
23  #y0 = 10.0, 1.0, 1.0
24  #y0 = 5.0, 5.0, 5.0
25  t             = np.linspace (0,  20,  4000)
26  solution = odeint(calculate , y0, t, args = (a, b, c))
27  X, Y, Z = solution [:,0],  solution [:,1],  solution [:,2]

30  ################## main ##########################
31  # xy Plot of ODE
32  fig_a  = plt . figure ()
33  ax_a  = fig_a . add_subplot(111, title  ="XY")
34  ax_a. axis ("Off")
35  ax_a.plot (X, Y, "black")
36  fig_a . savefig (picname + "_XY.pdf", bbox_inches='tight ' )

38  # xz Plot of ODE
39  fig_b  = plt . figure ()
```

```
40    ax_b  = fig_b . add_subplot(111, title ="XZ")
41    ax_b. axis ("Off")
42    ax_b. plot (X, Z, "black")
43    fig_b . savefig (picname + "_XZ.pdf", bbox_inches='tight ' )

45    # yz Plot of ODE
46    fig_c  = plt . figure ()
47    ax_c  = fig_c . add_subplot(111, title ="YZ")
48    ax_c. axis ("Off")
49    ax_c. plot (Y, Z, "black")
50    fig_c . savefig (picname + "_YZ.pdf", bbox_inches='tight ' )

52    # xyz 3D-Plot of ODE
53    fig_d  = plt . figure ()
54    ax_d  = fig_d . add_subplot(111, projection = "3d", title ="3d_"+ picname)
55    ax_d. set_xticklabels ([])
56    ax_d. set_yticklabels ([])
57    ax_d. set_zticklabels ([])
58    ax_d. plot (X, Y, Z, "black")
59    fig_d . savefig (picname + "_3d.pdf", bbox_inches='tight ' )

61    # Plot of xy, xz, yz and xyz 3D grafics
62    fig2  = plt . figure ()
63    ax2  = fig2 . add_subplot(221, title ="XY")
64    ax3  = fig2 . add_subplot(222, title ="XZ")
65    ax4  = fig2 . add_subplot(223, title ="YZ")
66    ax5  = fig2 . add_subplot(224, projection = "3d", title ="3d_"+ picname)
67    ax2. axis ("Off")
68    ax3. axis ("Off")
69    ax4. axis ("Off")
70    ax2. plot (X, Y, "black")
71    ax3. plot (X, Z, "black")
72    ax4. plot (Y, Z, "black")
73    ax5. set_xticklabels ([])
74    ax5. set_yticklabels ([])
75    ax5. set_zticklabels ([])
76    ax5. plot (X, Y, Z, "black")
77    fig2 . savefig (picname + "_4. pdf", bbox_inches='tight ' )
78    plt . show()
```

The complete Python programme shown here consists of two parts: the *calculate* method (line 13 to 19) and the actual main programme (from line 30). **The second part, the actual main program, always remains the same and unchanged.** [1] For other examples, other differential equations, one only needs to exchange the first part (and its parameters) to get a different computer graphic.

---

[1] Currently, the images are provided with headings of the coordinate designation! For computer graphics without a caption, the corresponding *subplot* command must be changed in the main program

```
1  import math
2  import numpy as np
3  import matplotlib. pyplot as plt
4  from mpl_toolkits. mplot3d import Axes3D
5  from scipy.integrate  import odeint

7  # Parameter
8  picname = "Lorenz_Standard"
9  a = 10
10 b = 28 # 28, 99.65, 100.5, 160, 350
11 c = 8.0/3.0
12 # basic equation
13 def calculate (u, t, a, b, c):
14     x, y, z = u
15     # Lorenz_Standard
16     dxdt = a*(y-x)
17     dydt = x*(b-z) - y
18     dzdt = x*y - c*z
19     return(dxdt, dydt, dzdt)

21 # start values and initialization
22 y0 = 0.1,  0.1,  0.1
23 #y0 = 10.0, 1.0, 1.0
24 #y0 = 5.0, 5.0, 5.0
25 t            = np.linspace (0,  20,  4000)
26 solution = odeint(calculate , y0, t, args = (a, b, c))
27 X, Y, Z = solution [:,0],   solution [:,1],   solution [:,2]
```

Looking more closely at the code, one can identify three main areas - numbered from 1 to 3.

- Area **1**
  This area always remains the same and defines the libraries used. These are either imported completely or individual parts are imported (*Axes3D, odeint*).

- Area **2**

  Includes lines 7 of # *parameters* up to line 19 *return(dxdt, dydt, dzdt)* (for this use case). Every differential equation, represented by the respective calculate method, needs starting parameters. In this case of the Lorenz equation, it is the three parameters a, b, c. In other differential equations, it may be necessary to specify more or fewer parameters. The exact names of these parameters must then be entered in the call to the solution routine (line 26)!

- Area **3**

  Deals with the settings necessary to call the numerical calculation of the differential equation system using the *odeint* subroutine.

The *odeint* library provides a set of algorithms for the solution of ordinary differential equations (ODEs), typically encountered in dynamical systems and many other scientific fields. *odeint* is written in C++ and can be used as an external library in Python.

Info   Info Odeint C++ Bibliothek ▷ `https://bit.ly/3OXnnqR`
             Odeint C++ Lorenz Beispiel ▷ `https://bit.ly/3yz38dz`

Before we turn to the details of Python and the central graphics library *matplotlib* in the next chapter, let us return once more to the standard Lorenz attractor programme already explained. As explained, the entire code consists of two parts. We will now show these two parts again, but not as code lists, but in the form of a *QR code*.

Info   QR code ▷ `https://bit.ly/3nP4LxP`

We use the QR code in this book so that you don't have to type out the examples, that you use for experimentation.

A QR code[2] (short for **Q**uick **R**esponse Code) is a two-dimensional code that can store and transmit information. It was developed in 1994 by

---

[2] The QRQR reader (https://bit.ly/3n9MnTx) from Denso Wave supports the following codes:

2D codes: QR Code models 1 and 2 (GS1 format),Micro QR Code, FrameQR, and MapQR

Barcodes: AN-13, EAN-8 (JAN-13 and JAN-8), UPC-A, UPC-E, and UPC/EAN with add-ons

the Japanese company Denso Wave and is now widely used in many applications. Thanks to automatic error correction, this method is very robust and therefore widely used. QR codes consist of black and white

QR Code Reader

Figure 2.1 Logo QRQR Code App

pixels that form a pattern. These patterns are arranged so that they can be recognized by a QR code scanner.

To read a QR code, you need a smartphone, a tablet or a QR code scanner. Most smartphones today already have an integrated QR code scanner function. When you capture the QR code with the scanner, you receive the information stored in it. You can now send this information to yourself by email and copy and paste it into the software you are using.

Info QRQR AppStore (IOS) ▷ https://r.qrqrq.com/MKp88Eu1
QRQR Google Play (Android) ▷ https://r.qrqrq.com/VIYo8yhF

Simply have the code translated and - voilà - you will receive the desired desired computer graphics.

There are a very large number of QR code apps for smartphones. We use the *QRQR* scanner from the company Denso Wave, which invented the QR code process in 1994. You can find this app under the name *QRQR* in the respective smartphone portals. It is free to use and free of annoying advertising. If you don't want to type out the source code

Figure 2.2   QRQR Code-App für Android GooglePlay und Apple IOS

of the programs, you can simply scan the two parts of the QR code[3] using your cell phone or tablet and send it to yourself by e-mail. The two parts must of course then be put together in a text editor. The overall file generated in this way can then be created using the software development environment *Thonny* to generate the images.

After this first scan of both parts of the QR code, you only ever need the first part of the code archive (chapter 4).

---

[3]   QR code: left side part 1, right side part 2
Part 1 of the central code is always replaced
Part 2 of the central code remains unchanged in each case

It is particularly important to ensure after scanning the QR code and accessing the source code of the programming, that the indentation structure of the entire Python code is displayed correctly (even after transmission by e-mail). It is quite possible that the selected QR code scanning software via mobile or tablet app does not correctly determine the correct indentation structure of the Python code!

Part 1 (calculate)   Part 2 (main)

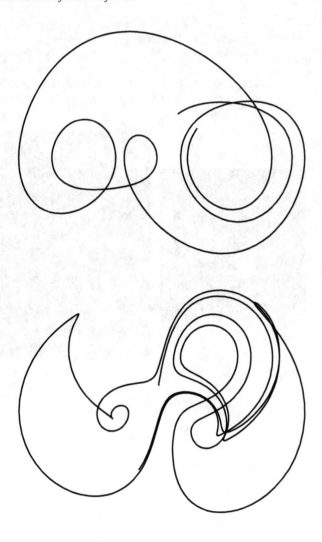

3 Python and the *matplotlib* library

Python is an imperative script programming language that supports all major operating systems and features an extensive, extensible standard library.

Info   Python Programming Language ▷ https://bit.ly/3nx9pAi

For Python, you would actually have to install the Python interpreter and other external libraries on many computers. However, there is a very elegant software development environment (IDE) from the Finnish University of Tartu that contains everything needed for the current Python version.

Info   Development environment IDE ▷ https://bit.ly/3yN2w4x

Den Editor *Thonny* kann man für alle gängigen Betriebssysteme Windows, Linux, MacOSX herunterladen:

Info   Info Thonny IDE ▷ https://bit.ly/3IdTbpd

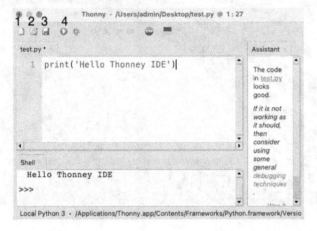

Figure 3.1   The first program

After downloading and starting the Thonny IDE, the editor window appears. There are two large areas in the editor window. The upper area is for coding Python commands. The lower area, called *Shell*, is the output area for text output. Graphic outputs are displayed in additional graphic windows or saved on the hard disk if programmed accordingly. At the top of the editor window, you can see various symbols:

- Area **1**
  The icon marked with number 1 is used to create a new file. Python programs are stored in individual files that can be opened and executed.
- Area **2**
  Clicking on the folder symbol opens an already existing Python file, which can then be edited or executed in the editor.
- Area **3**
  A click on the diskette symbol saves the current program.
- Area **4**
  The arrow symbol starts the program for execution. The result is displayed in the *Shell* - the output window or in the graphics window.
  (The stop symbol stops the program immediately).

Python modules are installed and managed directly within Thonny.

External libraries like *NumPy*, *SciPy* or *Matplotlib* can therefore be easily added. If you need functions provided by *NumPy*, *SciPy* or *Matplotlib* from an external module, you have to install these modules separately, because they are not included in the standard library. For our algorithms, these 3 libraries are absolutely necessary!

Info   Python 3 Standard Library ▷ https://bit.ly/3bzDyfw

The installation of the additional modules is done via the menu *Tools > Manage packages...*:

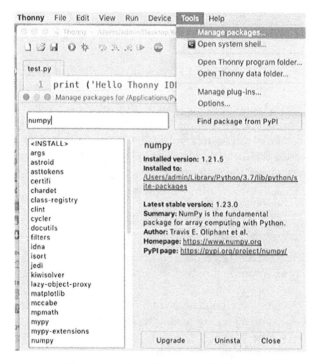

Figure 3.2   Installing external libraries

If you now enter our sample program for the Lorenz attractor into the editor, the result looks like this with several graphic windows.

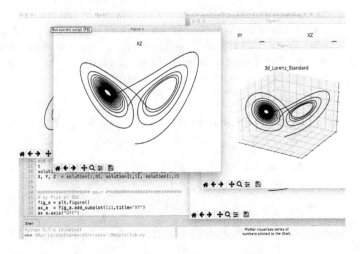

Figure 3.3 Standard Lorenz Python version

The content of the graphic windows is saved as PDF file. [1] The operation and use of the Thonny IDE is relatively simple. We recommend that you learn more about Thonny by watching *YouTube videos* on the internet. It is now time to briefly look at the framework and the settings for the *matplotlib* library.

```
1    import math
2    import numpy as np
3    import matplotlib. pyplot  as plt
4    from mpl_toolkits. mplot3d import Axes3D
5    from scipy.integrate   import odeint
```

The necessary external libraries are defined at the very beginning of the program. [2]

- Line **1**:
  Import all functions from math. The functions can only be used with a prefixed module name: *math.sqrt(...)*
- Line **2**:
  Import all functions from NumPy. The functions can be used here with an abbreviated module name: *np.linspace(...)*

---

[1] The file type .PDF can also be changed: .png, .jpg etc.
[2] There is another function for the solution of differential equations called *solve_ip*:
https://bit.ly/3OXSr9V

- Line **3**:
  Import all functions from *matplotlib.pyplot*. The functions can be used here with an abbreviated module name: *plt.subplot(...)* matplotlib.pyplot is a collection of functions. Each pyplot function makes some change to a figure.

- Line **4**:
  Toolkits are collections of application-specific functions that extend matplotlib. Creating 3D diagrams is made possible with the *mplot3d toolkit* and *Axes3D*.

- Line **5**:
  The open-source software environment *SciPy* provides the module *odeint* for the numerical solution of differential equations.

The main programme using the libraries mentioned looks like this:

```
30   ################### main ###########################
31   # xy Plot of ODE
32   fig_a = plt.figure ()
33   ax_a  = fig_a .add_subplot(111, title ="XY")
34   ax_a.axis ("Off")
35   ax_a.plot (X, Y, "black")
36   fig_a .savefig (picname + "_XY.pdf", bbox_inches='tight ' )

38   # xz Plot of ODE
39   fig_b = plt.figure ()
40   ax_b  = fig_b .add_subplot(111, title ="XZ")
41   ax_b.axis ("Off")
42   ax_b.plot (X, Z, "black")
43   fig_b .savefig (picname + "_XZ.pdf", bbox_inches='tight ' )

45   # yz Plot of ODE
46   fig_c  = plt.figure ()
47   ax_c  = fig_c .add_subplot(111, title ="YZ")
48   ax_c.axis ("Off")
49   ax_c.plot (Y, Z, "black")
50   fig_c .savefig (picname + "_YZ.pdf", bbox_inches='tight ' )

52   # xyz 3D-Plot of ODE
53   fig_d = plt.figure ()
54   ax_d  = fig_d .add_subplot(111, projection  = "3d", title ="3d_"+ picname)
55   ax_d.set_xticklabels ([])
56   ax_d.set_yticklabels ([])
57   ax_d.set_zticklabels ([])
58   ax_d.plot (X, Y, Z, "black")
59   fig_d .savefig (picname + "_3d.pdf", bbox_inches='tight ' )

61   # Plot of xy, xz, yz and xyz 3D grafics
62   fig2  = plt.figure ()
63   ax2  = fig2 .add_subplot(221, title ="XY")
64   ax3  = fig2 .add_subplot(222, title ="XZ")
65   ax4  = fig2 .add_subplot(223, title ="YZ")
66   ax5  = fig2 .add_subplot(224, projection  = "3d", title ="3d_"+ picname)
```

```
67    ax2. axis ("Off")
68    ax3. axis ("Off")
69    ax4. axis ("Off")
70    ax2. plot (X, Y, "black")
71    ax3. plot (X, Z, "black")
72    ax4. plot (Y, Z, "black")
73    ax5. set_xticklabels ([])
74    ax5. set_yticklabels ([])
75    ax5. set_zticklabels ([])
76    ax5. plot (X, Y, Z, "black")
77    fig2 . savefig (picname + "_4. pdf", bbox_inches='tight ' )
78    plt . show()
```

A total of 5 graphics are generated. The corresponding algorithms
each start with the label comment:
line 31 (xy plot), line 38 (xz plot), line 45 (yz plot), line 52 (xyz 3D plot),
line 61 (4 plots). The individual drawings - labelled figures in matplotlib
- are each created with the command

```
fig_a = plt.figure(), fig_b = plt.figure(),
fig_c = plt.figure(), fig_d = plt.figure()
```

defined for the individual drawings.
    The drawing for the four graphics in one picture is:

```
fig2 = plt.figure().
```

Since *matplotlib* provides a coordinate and axis related graphics
package, many labels can be made regarding the coordinate system
and the axis labels. Since we are only interested in the pure graphics,
we have switched off all additional labels. The only labelling is the
name, the designation. Please inform yourself about these details in the
documentation of the library *matplotlib*. Experiment with the respective
commands (switching on or off the respective lines).
    pyplot.subplots offers the possibility to generate an image and a grid
of subplots with a single call. Please experiment with the commands
shown here as well.

Info   matplotlib Tutorial ▷ https://bit.ly/3a7YBpp
                mplot3d-Toolkit ▷ https://bit.ly/3bEXDRH
                matplotlib subplot ▷ https://bit.ly/3OX6TPn

And please always remember that two parts (of QR codes[3]) must be
gathered to form a complete program!

---

[3]   QR-code: left side part 1, right side part 2
       Part 1 of the central code, is exchanged each time
       Part 2 of the central code, remains unchanged in each case

Part 1 (calculate)   Part 2 (main)

The Python programs[4] generate plots for differential equations with the parameters a, b, c, for example. The type of differential equation is defined by the basic equation, which contains the derivatives of the variables x, y and z as a function of the values of x, y and z and the fixed parameters a, b, c. The differential equation is calculated with solved numerically using the scipy.integrate odeint solver. The solutions are then displayed in various diagrams. In total, there are different diagrams[5], each showing the relationship between different variables x, y and z. The first diagram shows the relationship between x and y on a two-dimensional plane, the second diagram shows the relationship between x and z. The third diagram shows the relationship between y and z. The fourth diagram shows a three-dimensional representation of x, y and z. The diagrams are created using matplotlib.pyplot and mpl_toolkits.mplot3d. Each diagram is generated in a separate figure and the plots it contains are displayed as subplots. The diagrams are saved as PDF and PNG files. The names of the files are defined by the variable name *picname* and an additional suffix.

---

4   as QR code consisting of two parts
5   Please refer to the examples in the next chapter

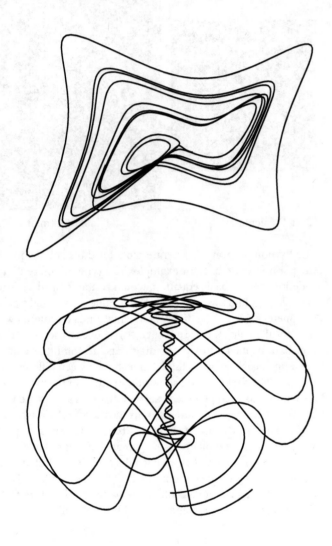

4 Images of the iterative fractals

In this chapter, you will find the images of the recipes, whose exact description is provided in the chapter *code archive of the iterative fractals*. The pictures show the result when we combine the three simple projections (x, y-plane, x, z-plane, y, z-plane) as well as a pseudo 3D oblique representation in one drawing. We now show three-dimensional attractors in many small pictures numbered from #01 to #82 (with two-digit numbers). The names indicate the discoverers of these formulae. In the appendix, the sources from which the formulas are taken are given for some of them. And now have fun trying and experimenting for images from the universe of computer graphics.

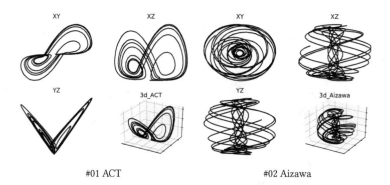

#01 ACT   #02 Aizawa

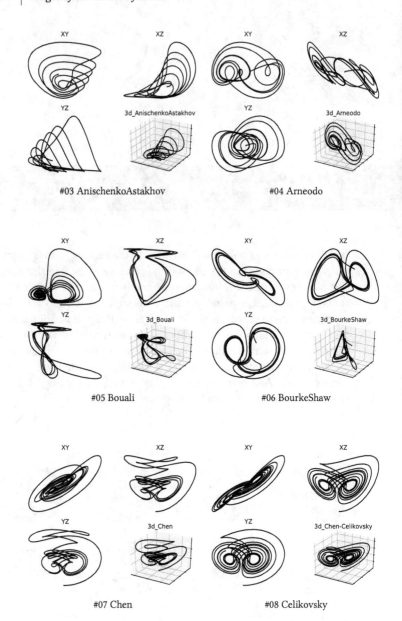

#03 AnischenkoAstakhov

#04 Arneodo

#05 Bouali

#06 BourkeShaw

#07 Chen

#08 Celikovsky

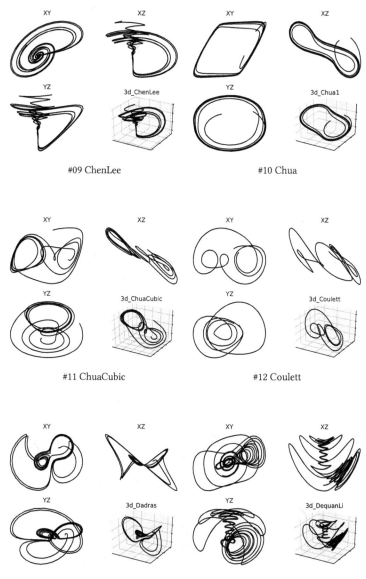

#09 ChenLee

#10 Chua

#11 ChuaCubic

#12 Coulett

#13 Dadras

#14 DequanLi

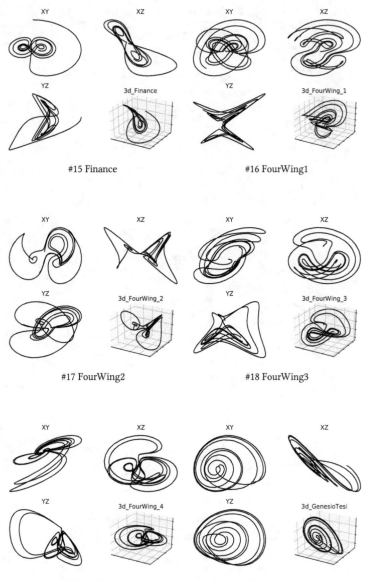

#15 Finance

#16 FourWing1

#17 FourWing2

#18 FourWing3

#19 FourWing4

#20 GenesioTesi

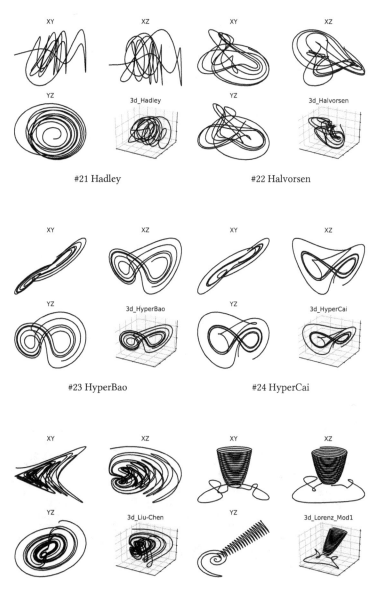

#21 Hadley

#22 Halvorsen

#23 HyperBao

#24 HyperCai

#25 Liu-Chen

#26 LorenzMod1

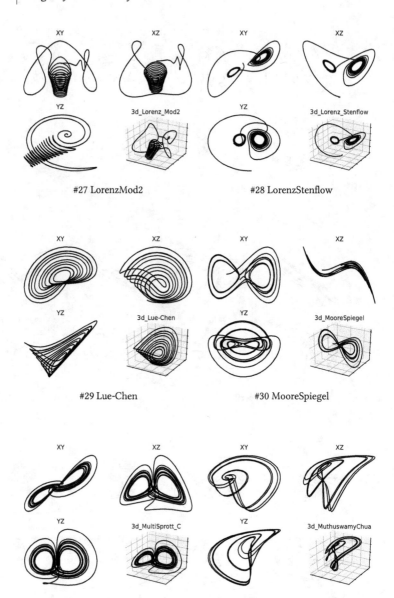

#27 LorenzMod2

#28 LorenzStenflow

#29 Lue-Chen

#30 MooreSpiegel

#31 MultiSprottC

#32 MuthuswamyChua

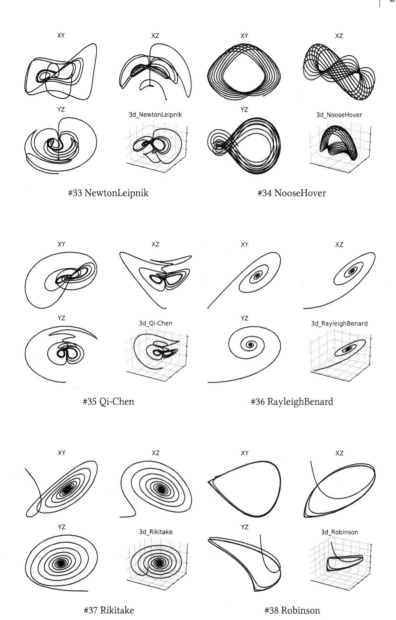

#33 NewtonLeipnik

#34 NooseHover

#35 Qi-Chen

#36 RayleighBenard

#37 Rikitake

#38 Robinson

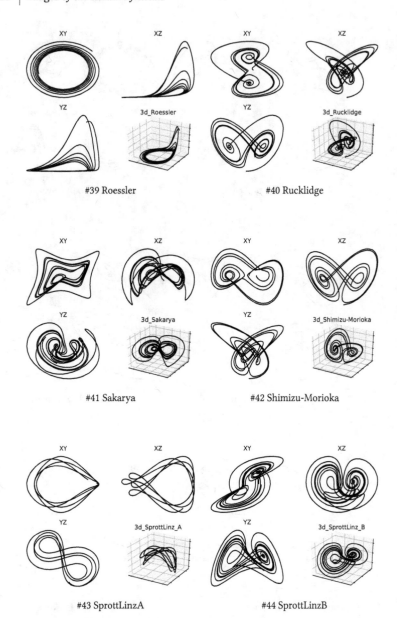

#39 Roessler   #40 Rucklidge

#41 Sakarya   #42 Shimizu-Morioka

#43 SprottLinzA   #44 SprottLinzB

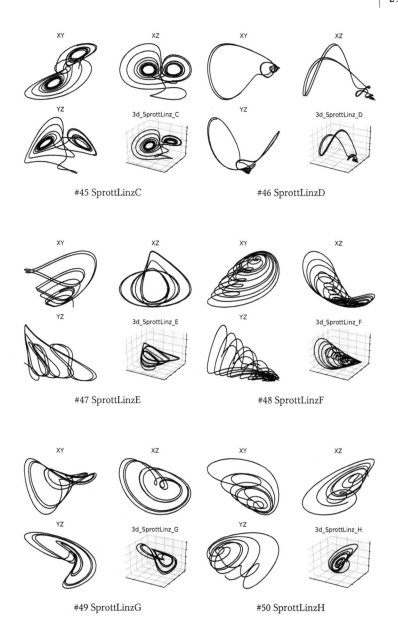

#45 SprottLinzC

#46 SprottLinzD

#47 SprottLinzE

#48 SprottLinzF

#49 SprottLinzG

#50 SprottLinzH

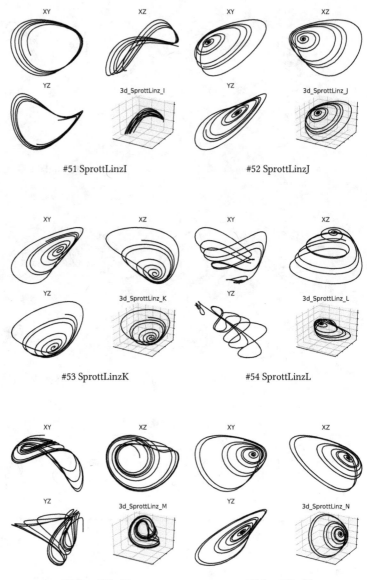

#51 SprottLinzI

#52 SprottLinzJ

#53 SprottLinzK

#54 SprottLinzL

#55 SprottLinzM

#56 SprottLinzN

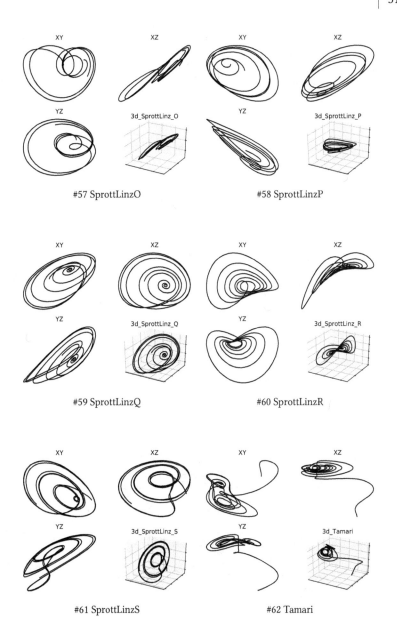

#57 SprottLinzO

#58 SprottLinzP

#59 SprottLinzQ

#60 SprottLinzR

#61 SprottLinzS

#62 Tamari

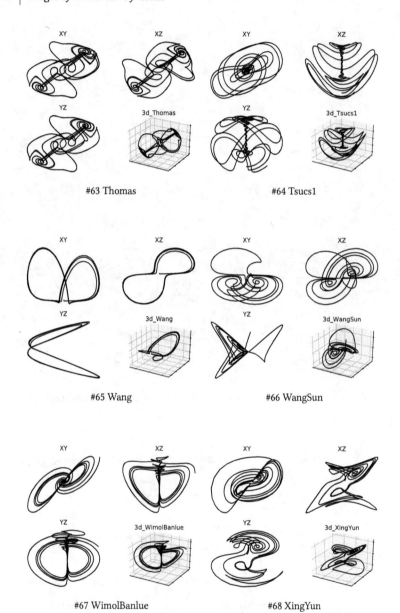

#63 Thomas

#64 Tsucs1

#65 Wang

#66 WangSun

#67 WimolBanlue

#68 XingYun

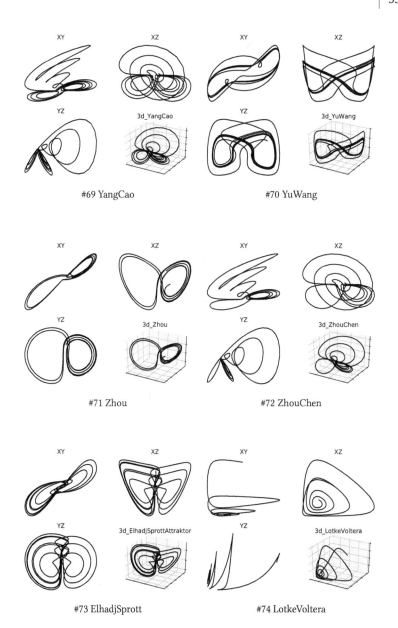

#69 YangCao

#70 YuWang

#71 Zhou

#72 ZhouChen

#73 ElhadjSprott

#74 LotkeVoltera

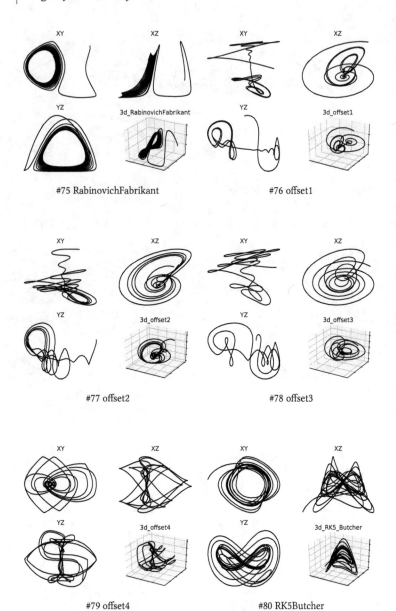

#75 RabinovichFabrikant

#76 offset1

#77 offset2

#78 offset3

#79 offset4

#80 RK5Butcher

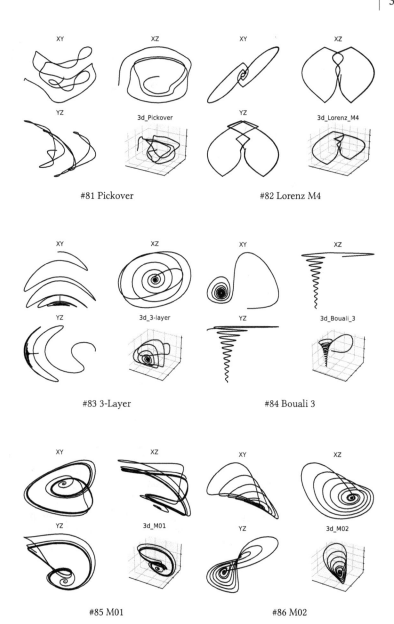

#81 Pickover

#82 Lorenz M4

#83 3-Layer

#84 Bouali 3

#85 M01

#86 M02

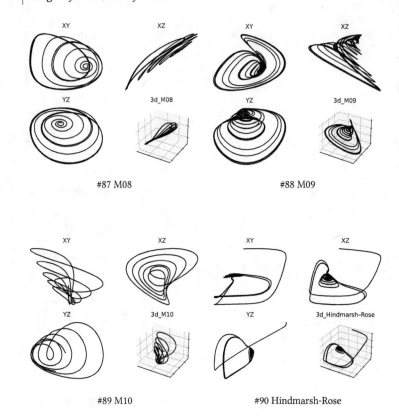

#87 M08

#88 M09

#89 M10

#90 Hindmarsh-Rose

Currently, the images are provided with headings of the coordinate designation! For computer graphics without a caption, the corresponding *subplot* command must be changed in the main program. Compare this with the Lorenz attractor example program on page 5. The plot commands for the headings are still present there. Another example program (Thomas attractor) WITHOUT coordinate headings can be found on page 131.

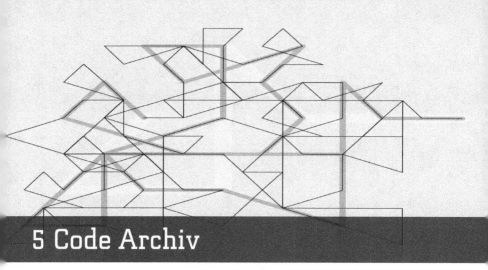

5 Code Archiv

In this chapter *CodeArchive* you will now find all subroutines/methods of type `calculate` for generating the iterative fractals. The selected subroutine (calculate) must be replaced in the central Python framework program (main). Next to the displayed code, you will find the corresponding QR code so that you can easily assemble the desired framework programme via *copy and paste...*

Part 1 (calculate)   Part 2 (main)

```python
import numpy as np
import matplotlib.pyplot as plt
from mpl_toolkits.mplot3d import Axes3D
from scipy.integrate import odeint

# Parameter
picname ="ACT"
a = 1.8
b = -0.07
d = 1.5
m = 0.02

# basic equation
def calculate (u, t, a, b, d, m):
    x, y, z = u
    # ACT
    dxdt = a*(x-y)
    dydt = -4*a*y+x*z+m*pow(x,3)
    dzdt = -d*a*z+x*y+b*z*z
    return(dxdt, dydt, dzdt)

# start values and initialization
y0 = 0.1, 0.1, 0.1
t = np.linspace(0, 30, 2000)
solution = odeint(calculate , y0, t, args = (a, b, d, m))
X, Y, Z = solution [:,0], solution [:,1], solution [:,2]
```

Gelli MBSS Kumar und V Chandrasekaran. *A generic framework for robust image encryption using multiple chaotic flows.* In: International Journal of Computational Cognition) 8.3 (2010), p. 13, #1 ACT
url: https://bit.ly/3rVdhef

```python
import numpy as np
import matplotlib.pyplot as plt
from mpl_toolkits.mplot3d import Axes3D
from scipy.integrate import odeint

# Parameter
picname ="Aizawa"
a = 0.95
b = 0.7
c = 0.6
d = 3.5
e = 0.25
f = 0.1

# basic equation
def calculate (u, t, a, b, c, d, e, f):
    x, y, z = u
    # Aizawa
    dxdt = (z-b)*x - d*y
    dydt = d*x + (z-b)*y
    short = (x*x + y*y)*(1+e*z) + f*z*pow(x,3)
    dzdt = c + a*z - pow(z,3)/3 - short
    return(dxdt, dydt, dzdt)

# start values and initialization
y0 = -1.0, 0.9, 1.0
t = np.linspace (0, 40, 2000)
solution = odeint(calculate , y0, t, args = (a, b, c, d, e, f))
X, Y, Z = solution [:,0], solution [:,1], solution [:,2]
```

XY   XZ

YZ   3d_Aizawa

Yoji Aizawa und Tatsuya Uezu. *Global aspects of the dissipative dynamical systems. II: Periodic and chaotic responses in the forced Lorenz system.* In: Progress of Theoretical Physics 68.6 (1982), S. 1864–1879, #2 Aizawa
url: https://doi.org/10.1143/PTP.68.1864

```python
import numpy as np
import matplotlib.pyplot as plt
from mpl_toolkits.mplot3d import Axes3D
from scipy.integrate import odeint

# Parameter
picname ="AnischenkoAstakhov"
m = 1.2
g = 0.5

def f(x):
    if (x > 0):
        return 1
    else:
        return 0

# basic equation
def calculate (u, t, m, g):
    x, y, z = u
    # AnischenkAstakhov
    dxdt = m*x+y-x*z
    dydt = -x
    dzdt = -g*z+g*f(x)*x*x
    return(dxdt, dydt, dzdt)

# start values and initialization
y0 = 1.0, 1.0, 1.0
t = np.linspace (0, 50, 2000)
solution = odeint(calculate , y0, t, args = (m, g))
X, Y, Z = solution [:,0], solution [:,1], solution [:,2]
```

XY

XZ

YZ

3d_AnischenkoAstakhov

Vadim S. Anishchenko und Galina I. Strelkova. Irregular Attractors. In: Discrete Dynamics in Nature and Society 2 (1998), p. 252749, #3,#98 Anishchenko-Astakhov url: https://doi.org/10.1155/S1026022698000041 / url: https://bit.ly/3cSYsEA

```python
import numpy as np
import matplotlib. pyplot as  plt
from mpl_toolkits. mplot3d import Axes3D
from scipy.integrate  import odeint

# Parameter
picname ="Arneodo"
a = -5.5
b = 3.5
c = -1.0

# basic equation
def calculate (u, t, a, b,c):
    x, y, z = u
    # Arneodo
    dxdt = y
    dydt = z
    dzdt = -a*x -b*y -z + c*pow(x,3)
    return(dxdt, dydt, dzdt)

# start values and initialization
y0 = 0.1,  0 , 0
#y0 = -1.0, 0.9, 1.0
t = np.linspace (0, 40, 2000)
solution = odeint(calculate , y0, t, args = (a, b,c))
X, Y, Z = solution [:,0],  solution [:,1],  solution [:,2]
```

XY XZ

YZ 3d_Arneodo

Vaidyanathan, Sundarapandian. Output regulation of Arneodo-Coullet chaotic system. International Conference on Computer Science and Information Technology. Springer, Berlin, Heidelberg, 2011, #4 Arneodo
url: https://shorturl.at/grJlK

```python
import numpy as np
import matplotlib. pyplot as plt
from mpl_toolkits. mplot3d import Axes3D
from scipy.integrate  import odeint

# Parameter
picname = "Bouali_1"
a = 0.3
b = 1.0

# basic equation
def calculate (u, t, a, b):
    x, y, z = u
    # Bouali_1
    dxdt = x*(4-y) + a*z
    dydt = -y*(1-x*x)
    dzdt = -x*(1.5  - b*z) - 0.05*z
    return(dxdt, dydt, dzdt)

# start values and initialization
y0 = 1, 0.1 , 0.1
#y0 = -1.0, 0.9, 1.0
t  = np.linspace (0, 50, 3000)
solution = odeint(calculate , y0, t, args = (a, b))
X, Y, Z = solution [:,0],   solution [:,1],   solution [:,2]
```

Safieddine Bouali. A novel strange attractor with a stretched loop. In: Nonlinear Dynamics 70.4 (2012), p. 23752381, #5 Bouali
url: https://bit.ly/3cV40Pd

```python
import numpy as np
import matplotlib. pyplot  as  plt
from mpl_toolkits. mplot3d import Axes3D
from scipy.integrate  import odeint

# Parameter
picname = "BourkeShaw"
a = 10
b = 4.272

# basic equation
def calculate (u, t, a, b):
    x, y, z = u
    # BourkeShaw
    dxdt = -a*(x+y)
    dydt = -y - a*x*z
    dzdt = a*x*y + b
    return(dxdt, dydt, dzdt)

# start values and initialization
#y0 = 1, 0 , 0
y0 = 0.5, 0.5, 0.5
t = np.linspace (0, 10, 2000)
#t = np.linspace(0, 20, 2000)
solution = odeint(calculate , y0, t, args = (a, b))
X, Y, Z = solution [:,0],  solution [:,1],  solution [:,2]
```

XY

YZ

XZ

3d_BourkeShaw

Robert Shaw. Strange attractors, chaotic behavior, and information flow. In: Zeitschrift für Naturforschung A 36.1 (1981), p. 80–112, #6 Burke-Shaw
url: https://doi.org/10.1515/zna-1981-0115

```python
import numpy as np
import matplotlib.pyplot as plt
from mpl_toolkits.mplot3d import Axes3D
from scipy.integrate import odeint

# Parameter
picname = "Chen"
a = 35      # 36
b = 2.66    # 3
c = 28      # 20

# basic equation
def calculate (u, t, a, b, c):
    x, y, z = u
    # Chen
    dxdt = a*(y - x)
    dydt = (c - a)*x - x*z + c*y
    dzdt = x*y - b*z
    return(dxdt, dydt, dzdt)

# start values and initialization
y0 = 1.0,  1.0,  1.0
#y0 = -3, 2, 20
#y0 = -5, 5, 20
t = np.linspace(0, 5, 2000)
#t = np.linspace(0, 10, 2000)
solution = odeint(calculate, y0, t, args = (a, b, c))
X, Y, Z = solution [:,0],  solution [:,1],  solution [:,2]
```

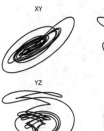
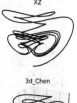

Tetsushi Ueta u. a. Bifurcation and chaos in coupled BVP oscillators. In: International Journal of Bifurcation and Chaos 14.04 (2004), p. 1305–1324, #7 Chen
url: https://doi.org/10.1142/S0218127404009983

```python
import numpy as np
import matplotlib.pyplot as plt
from mpl_toolkits.mplot3d import Axes3D
from scipy.integrate import odeint

# Parameter
picname = "Chen-Celikovsky"
a = 36
b = 3
c = 20

# basic equation
def calculate (u, t, a, b, c):
    x, y, z = u
    # Chen-Celikovsky
    dxdt = a*(y - x)
    dydt = - x*z + c*y
    dzdt = x*y - b*z
    return(dxdt, dydt, dzdt)

# start values and initialization
y0 = 1.0, 1.0, 1.0
#y0 = -3, 2, 20
#y0 = -5, 5, 20
t = np.linspace(0, 10, 2000)
solution = odeint(calculate , y0, t, args = (a, b, c))
X, Y, Z = solution [:,0], solution [:,1], solution [:,2]
```

XY   XZ

YZ   3d_Chen-Celikovsky

Jinhu Lü und Guanrong Chen. A new chaotic attractor coined. In: International Journal of Bifurcation and chaos 12.03 (2002), p. 659–661, #8 Chen-Celikovsky url: https://doi.org/10.1142/S0218127402004620 | url: https://bit.ly/3xahrmm

```python
import numpy as np
import matplotlib.pyplot as plt
from mpl_toolkits.mplot3d import Axes3D
from scipy.integrate import odeint

# Parameter
picname = "ChenLee"
a = 5
b = -10
c = -0.38

# basic equation
def calculate (u, t, a, b, c):
    x, y, z = u
    # ChenLee
    dxdt = a*x - y*z
    dydt = b*y + x*z
    dzdt = c*z + x*(y/3)
    return(dxdt, dydt, dzdt)

# start values and initialization
#y0 = 1.0, 1.0, 1.0
#y0 = -3, 2, 20
y0 = -5, 5, 20
t = np.linspace (0, 30, 2000)
solution = odeint(calculate , y0, t, args = (a, b, c))
X, Y, Z = solution [:,0],    solution [:,1],    solution [:,2]
```

XY

XZ

YZ

3d_ChenLee

Yin Li und Biao Li. Chaos control and projective synchronization of a chaotic Chen-Lee system. In: Chinese Journal of Physics 47.3 (2009), p. 261–270, #9 Chen-Lee

```python
import numpy as np
import matplotlib.pyplot as plt
from mpl_toolkits.mplot3d import Axes3D
from scipy.integrate import odeint

# Parameter
picname = "Chua1"
a = 15.6
b = 1.0
c = 25.58
d = -1
e = 0

def calculate (u, t, a, b, c, d, e):
    x, y, z = u
    # Chua1
    short = (abs(x + 1) - abs(x - 1))
    gx    = e * x + (d + e) * short
    dxdt = a * (y - x - gx)
    dydt = b * (x - y + z)
    dzdt = -c * y
    return(dxdt, dydt, dzdt)

# start values and initialization
y0 = 2.5, 1.0, 4.0
t  = np.linspace(0, 10, 2000)
#t = np.linspace(0, 20, 2000)
solution = odeint(calculate, y0, t, args = (a, b, c, d, e))
X, Y, Z = solution [:,0], solution [:,1], solution [:,2]
```

Chua, L. O. (1992). The genesis of Chua's circuit. Berkeley, CA, USA: Electronics Research Laboratory, College of Engineering, University of California, #10 Chua

```python
import numpy as np
import matplotlib.pyplot as plt
from mpl_toolkits.mplot3d import Axes3D
from scipy.integrate import odeint

# Parameter
picname = "Chua2"
a = 15.6
b = 1.0
c = 25.58
d = -1
e = 0

# Chua2
def calculate (u, t, a, b, c):
    x, y, z = u
    # Chua
    short = (abs(x + 1) - abs(x - 1))
    gx   = e * x + (d + e) * short
    dxdt = a * (y - x - gx)
    dydt = b * (x - y + z)
    dzdt = -c * y
    return(dxdt, dydt, dzdt)

# start values and initialization
y0 = 1.8, 1.3, 1
#y0 = 1, 1, 1
#y0 = 2.5, 1.0, 4.0
t = np.linspace(0, 10, 2000)
solution = odeint(calculate, y0, t, args = (a, b, c))
X, Y, Z = solution [:,0], solution [:,1], solution [:,2]
```

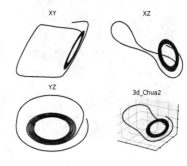

J.-M. Ginoux, Ch. Letellier und L.Chua.Topological analysis of chaotic solution of three-element memristive circuit, #10a Chua2
url: https://doi.org/10.1142/S0218127410027878

```python
import numpy as np
import matplotlib.pyplot as plt
from mpl_toolkits.mplot3d import Axes3D
from scipy.integrate import odeint

# Parameter
picname = "ChuaCubic"
alpha = 10
beta = 16
c = -0.143

# basic equation
def calculate (u, t, alpha, beta, c):
    x, y, z = u
    # ChuaCubic
    dxdt = alpha * (y - pow(x,3)-c*x)
    dydt = x - y + z
    dzdt = -beta * y
    return(dxdt, dydt, dzdt)

# start values and initialization
y0 = 0.1, 0.1, 0.1
#y0 = 2.5, 1.0, 4.0
t = np.linspace (0, 20, 2000)
solution = odeint(calculate , y0, t, args = (alpha, beta, c))
X, Y, Z = solution [:,0],  solution [:,1],  solution [:,2]
```

XY XZ

YZ 3d_ChuaCubic

Teh-Lu Liao und Fu-Wei Chen. Control of Chua's circuit with a cubic nonlinearity via nonlinear linearization technique. In: Circuits, Systems and Signal Processing 17.6 (1998), p. 719–731, #11 Chua Cubic
url: https://doi.org/10.1007/BF01206572

```python
import numpy as np
import matplotlib.pyplot as plt
from mpl_toolkits.mplot3d import Axes3D
from scipy.integrate import odeint

# Parameter
picname ="Coulett"
a = 0.8
b = -1.1
c = -0.45
d = -1

# basic equation
def calculate (u, t, a, b, c, d):
    x, y, z = u
    # Coulett
    dxdt = y
    dydt = z
    dzdt = a*x+b*y+c*z+d*x*x*x
    return(dxdt, dydt, dzdt)

# start values and initialization
y0 = 0.1, 0.41, 0.31
t = np.linspace (0, 30, 2000)
#t = np.linspace(0, 100, 2000)
solution = odeint(calculate , y0, t, args = (a,b,c,d))
X, Y, Z = solution [:,0], solution [:,1], solution [:,2]
```

XY

XZ

YZ

3d_Coulett

On Solving Coullet System by Differential Transformation Method. In: Ankara University Journal of Science and Engineering 8.1 (2011), #12 Coullet
url: https://bit.ly/3uWD1w1

```python
import numpy as np
import matplotlib. pyplot  as  plt
from mpl_toolkits. mplot3d import Axes3D
from scipy.integrate  import odeint

# Parameter
picname ="Dadras"
p = 3
q = 2.7
r = 1.7
s = 2
e = 9

# basic equation
def calculate (u,  t,  p,q,r,s,e):
    x,  y,  z = u
    # Dadras
    dxdt = y-p*x+q*y*z
    dydt = r*y-x*z+z
    dzdt = s*x*y-e*z
    return(dxdt,  dydt,  dzdt)

# start values and initialization
y0 = 0.1,   0.1,   0.1
t  = np.linspace (0,   30,  3000)
solution  = odeint(calculate ,   y0,  t,   args = (p,q,r,s,e))
X,  Y,  Z = solution [:,0],   solution [:,1],   solution [:,2]
```

XY XZ

YZ 3d_Dadras

Sarasu Pakiriswamy und Sundarapandian Vaidyanathan. Active Controller Design for the Generalized Projective Synchronization Of Three-Scroll Chaotic Systems. In: International Journal of Advanced Information Technology (IJAIT) 2 (2012), #13 Dadras url: https://bit.ly/3oYoGeL

```python
import numpy as np
import matplotlib.pyplot as plt
from mpl_toolkits.mplot3d import Axes3D
from scipy.integrate import odeint

# Parameter
picname ="DequanLi"
a = 40
c = 1.833
d = 0.16
e = 0.65
k = 55
f = 20

# basic equation
def calculate (u, t, a,c,d,e,k,f):
    x, y, z = u
    # DequanLi
    dxdt = a*(y-x)+d*x*z
    dydt = k*x+f*y-x*z
    dzdt = c*z+x*y-e*x*x
    return(dxdt, dydt, dzdt)

# start values and initialization
y0 = 0.349, 0.0, -0.16
t = np.linspace(0, 3, 2000)
solution = odeint(calculate, y0, t, args = (a,c,d,e,k,f))
X, Y, Z = solution [:,0], solution [:,1], solution [:,2]
```

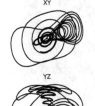

Christophe Letellier und Robert Gilmore. Poincar'e sections for a new three-dimensional toroidal attractor. In: Journal of Physics A: Mathematical and Theoretical 42.1 (2008), p. 015101, #14 DequanLi
url: https://doi.org/10.1088/1751-8113/42/1/015101 | url: https://bit.ly/3uWCIBn

```
import numpy as np
import matplotlib.pyplot as plt
from mpl_toolkits.mplot3d import Axes3D
from scipy.integrate import odeint

# Parameter
picname ="Finance"
a =  0.001
b =  0.2
c =  1.1

# basic equation
def calculate (u, t, a, b, c):
    x, y, z = u
    # Finance
    dxdt = (1/ b-a)*x+z+x*y
    dydt = -b*y-(x*x)
    dzdt = -x-c*z
    return(dxdt, dydt, dzdt)

# start values and initialization
y0 = 0.1,  0.0,  0.0
t  = np.linspace (0,  50,  2000)
#t = np.linspace(0, 100, 3000)
solution = odeint(calculate , y0, t, args = (a, b, c))
X, Y, Z = solution [:,0],   solution [:,1],   solution [:,2]
```

XY

XZ

YZ

3d_Finance

Sundarapandian Vaidyanathan u. a. A new finance chaotic system, its electronic circuit realization, passivity based synchronization and an application to voice encryption. In: Nonlinear Engineering 8.1 (2019), p. 193–205, #15 Finance url: https://doi.org/10.1515/nleng-2018-0012

```python
import numpy as np
import matplotlib.pyplot as plt
from mpl_toolkits.mplot3d import Axes3D
from scipy.integrate import odeint

# Parameter
picname ="FourWing_1"
a = 4
b = 6
c = 10
d = 5
k = 1

# basic equation
def calculate (u, t, a, b, c, d , k):
    x, y, z = u
    # FourWing_1
    dxdt = a*x-b*y*z
    dydt = -c*y+x*z
    dzdt = k*x-d*z+x*y
    return(dxdt, dydt, dzdt)

# start values and initialization
y0 = 0.1, 0.1, 0.1
t = np.linspace(0, 10, 2000)
solution = odeint(calculate , y0, t, args = (a,b,c,d,k))
X, Y, Z = solution [:,0], solution [:,1], solution [:,2]
```

XY

XZ

YZ

3d_FourWing_1

Dong En-Zeng u. a. A novel four-wing chaotic attractor generated from a three-dimensional quadratic autonomous system. In: Chinese Physics B 18.7 (2009), p. 2680, #16 FourWing 1
url: https://doi.org/10.1088/1674-1056/18/7/010

```python
import numpy as np
import matplotlib. pyplot as plt
from mpl_toolkits. mplot3d import Axes3D
from scipy.integrate import odeint

# Parameter
picname ="FourWing_2"
a = -14
b = 5
c = 1
d = 16
e = -43
f = 1

# basic equation
def calculate (u, t, a, b, c, d, e, f):
    x, y, z = u
    # FourWing_2
    dxdt = a*x+b*y+c*y*z
    dydt = d*y-x*z
    dzdt = e*z+f*x*y
    return(dxdt, dydt, dzdt)

# start values and initialization
y0 = 0.1, 0.1, 0.1
t = np.linspace (0, 3, 2000)
solution = odeint(calculate , y0, t, args = (a,b,c,d,e,f))
X, Y, Z = solution [:,0], solution [:,1], solution [:,2]
```

Zenghui Wang u. a. A generalized 3-D four-wing chaotic system. In: International Journal of Bifurcation and Chaos 19.11 (2009), p. 3841–3853, #17 FourWing 2 url: https://doi.org/10.1142/S0218127409025171

```python
import numpy as np
import matplotlib.pyplot as plt
from mpl_toolkits.mplot3d import Axes3D
from scipy.integrate import odeint

# Parameter
picname ="FourWing_3"
a = 4
b = 1

# basic equation
def calculate (u, t, a, b):
    x, y, z = u
    # FourWing_3
    dxdt = b*x+y+y*z
    dydt = y*z-a*x*z
    dzdt = -z-a*x*y+1
    return(dxdt, dydt, dzdt)

# start values and initialization
y0 = 0.1, 0.1, 0.1
t = np.linspace(0, 20, 2000)
solution = odeint(calculate, y0, t, args = (a, b))
X, Y, Z = solution [:,0], solution [:,1], solution [:,2]
```

XY

XZ

YZ

3d_FourWing_3

Akif Akgul, Chunbiao Li und Ihsan Pehlivan. Amplitude control analysis of a four-wing chaotic attractor, its electronic circuit designs and microcontroller-based random number generator. In: Journal of Circuits, Systems and Computers 26.12 (2017), p. 1750190, #18 FourWing 3
url: https://doi.org/10.1142/S0218126617501900

```
import numpy as np
import matplotlib.pyplot as plt
from mpl_toolkits.mplot3d import Axes3D
from scipy.integrate import odeint

# Parameter
picname ="FourWing_4"
a = 4
b = 2.5

# basic equation
def calculate (u, t, a, b):
    x, y, z = u
    # FourWing_4
    dxdt = b*x+y+y*z
    dydt = y*z-x*z
    dzdt = -z-a*x*y+1
    return(dxdt, dydt, dzdt)

# start values and initialization
y0 = 0.1, 0.1, 0.1
#t = np.linspace(0, 10, 2000)
t = np.linspace (0, 30, 2000)
#t = np.linspace(0, 100, 12000)
solution = odeint(calculate , y0, t, args = (a, b))
X, Y, Z = solution [:,0], solution [:,1], solution [:,2]
```

XY

XZ

YZ

3d_FourWing_4

Jinhu Lü, Guanrong Chen und Daizhan Cheng. A new chaotic system and beyond: the generalized Lorenz-like system. In: International Journal of Bifurcation and Chaos 14.05 (2004), p. 1507–1537, #19 Four Wing 4
url: https://doi.org/10.1142/S021812740401014X | url: https://bit.ly/3atNYKt

```python
import numpy as np
import matplotlib.pyplot as plt
from mpl_toolkits.mplot3d import Axes3D
from scipy.integrate import odeint

# Parameter
picname = "GenesioTesi"
a = 0.44
b = 1.1
c = 1.0

# basic equation
def calculate (u, t, a, b,c):
    x, y, z = u
    # GenesioTesi
    dxdt = y
    dydt = z
    dzdt = -c*x -b*y -a*z + x*x
    return(dxdt, dydt, dzdt)

# start values and initialization
y0 = 0.1, 0.1 , 0.1
t = np.linspace (0, 50, 2000)
#t = np.linspace(0, 100, 2000)
solution = odeint(calculate , y0, t, args = (a, b,c))
X, Y, Z = solution [:,0],  solution [:,1],  solution [:,2]
```

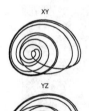

Jun-Guo, L. (2005). Chaotic dynamics and synchronization of fractional-order Genesio–Tesi systems. Chinese Physics, 14(8), 1517, #20 GenesioTesi

```
import numpy as np
import matplotlib. pyplot as plt
from mpl_toolkits. mplot3d import Axes3D
from scipy.integrate  import odeint

# Parameter
picname ="Hadley"
a = 0.2
b = 4
f = 8
g = 1

# basic equation
def calculate (u, t, a, b, f, g):
    x, y, z = u
    # Hadley
    dxdt =  -y*y-z*z-a*x+a*f
    dydt =  x*y-b*x*z-y+g
    dzdt =  b*x*y+x*z-z
    return(dxdt, dydt, dzdt)

# start values and initialization
y0 = 0.1,  0.0,  0.0
#t = np.linspace(0, 5, 2000)
t  = np.linspace (0,  15,  2000)
#t = np.linspace(0, 30, 2000)
#t = np.linspace(0, 50, 10000)
solution  = odeint(calculate , y0, t, args = (a,b,f,g))
X, Y, Z = solution [:,0],   solution [:,1],   solution [:,2]
```

Z. Zhao, J. Jian and W. Wang, Estimations of bounds and synchronization controlling for Hadley chaotic system, 2012 IEEE International Conference on Information Science and Technology, 2012, pp. 150-152, #21 Hadley
url: doi: 10.1109/ICIST.2012.6221626

```python
import numpy as np
import matplotlib. pyplot as plt
from mpl_toolkits. mplot3d import Axes3D
from scipy.integrate  import odeint

# Parameter
picname ="Halvorsen"
a = 1.4
b = 1

# basic equation
def calculate (u, t, a, b):
    x, y, z = u
    # Halvorsen
    dxdt = -a*x - 4*y - 4*z - y*y
    dydt = -a*y - 4*z - 4*x - z*z
    dzdt = -a*z - 4*x - 4*y - x*x
    return(dxdt, dydt, dzdt)

# start values and initialization
y0 = 1, 0 , 0
t  = np.linspace(0, 10, 2000)
#t = np.linspace(0, 30, 2000)
solution  = odeint(calculate , y0, t, args = (a, b))
X, Y, Z = solution [:,0],   solution [:,1],   solution [:,2]
```

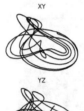

Vaidyanathan, S., Azar, A. T. (2016). Adaptive control and synchronization of Halvorsen circulant chaotic systems. In Advances in chaos theory and intelligent control (pp. 225-247). Springer, Cham, #22 Halvorsen

```python
import numpy as np
import matplotlib.pyplot as plt
from mpl_toolkits.mplot3d import Axes3D
from scipy.integrate import odeint

# Parameter
picname ="HyperBao"
a = 36
b = 3
c = 20
d = 0.1
k = 21

# basic equation
def calculate (u, t, a, b, c, d, k):
    x, y, z = u
    # HyperBao
    dxdt =  a*(y-x) + k*d
    dydt =  c*y - x*z
    dzdt =  x*y - b*z
    return(dxdt, dydt, dzdt)

# start values and initialization
y0 = 5, 8, 12
t  = np.linspace (0, 5, 2000)
#t = np.linspace(0, 15, 2000)
#t = np.linspace(0, 30, 8000)
solution  = odeint(calculate , y0, t, args = (a,b,c,d,k))
X, Y, Z = solution [:,0],  solution [:,1],  solution [:,2]
```

XY

XZ

YZ

3d_HyperBao

Xin Zhang u. a. A symmetric controllable hyperchaotic hidden attractor. In: Symmetry 12.4 (2020), p. 550, #23 Hyperchaotic Bao
url: https://doi.org/10.3390/sym12040550

```python
import numpy as np
import matplotlib.pyplot as plt
from mpl_toolkits.mplot3d import Axes3D
from scipy.integrate import odeint

# Parameter
picname ="HyperCai"
a = 27.5
b = 3
c = 19.3
d = 2.9
e = 3.3


# basic equation
def calculate (u, t, a, b, c, d, e):
    x, y, z = u
    # HyperCai
    dxdt = a*(y-x)
    dydt = b*x + c*y - x*z -e*x
    dzdt = -d*z + y*y
    return(dxdt, dydt, dzdt)


# start values and initialization
y0 = 5, 8, 12
t = np.linspace (0, 5, 2000)
#t = np.linspace(0, 15, 4000)
#t = np.linspace(0, 30, 8000)
solution = odeint(calculate , y0, t, args = (a,b,c,d,e))
X, Y, Z = solution [:,0], solution [:,1], solution [:,2]
```

XY   XZ

YZ   3d_HyperCai

Cai, G., Huang, J. (2007). A new finance chaotic attractor. International Journal of Nonlinear Science, 3(3), p.213-220, #24 HyperCai
url: https://bit.ly/3OxteTc

```python
import math
import numpy as np
import matplotlib.pyplot as plt
from mpl_toolkits.mplot3d import Axes3D
from scipy.integrate import odeint

# Parameter
picname ="Liu-Chen"
a = 2.4
b = -3.78
c = 14
d = -11
e = 4
f = 5.58
g = -1

# basic equation
def calculate (u, t, a, b, c,d,e,f,g):
    x, y, z = u
    # Liu-Chen
    dxdt = a*y + b*x + c*y*z
    dydt = d*y -z + e*x*z
    dzdt = f*z + g*x*y
    return(dxdt, dydt, dzdt)

# start values and initialization
y0 = 1, 3, 5
t = np.linspace(0, 20, 20000)
solution = odeint(calculate , y0, t, args = (a,b,c,d,e,f,g))
X, Y, Z = solution [:,0], solution [:,1], solution [:,2]
```

Yuhua Xu u. a. A new four-scroll chaotic attractor consisted of two-scroll transient chaotic and two-scroll ultimate chaotic. In: Mathematical Problems in Engineering 2012 (2012), #25 Liu-Chen
url: https://doi.org/10.1155/2012/438328 | url: https://bit.ly/3dCr05U

```python
import numpy as np
import matplotlib.pyplot as plt
from mpl_toolkits.mplot3d import Axes3D
from scipy.integrate import odeint

# Parameter
picname = "Lorenz_Mod1"
a = 0.1
b = 4
c = 14
d = 0.08
# basic equation
def calculate (u, t, a, b, c, d):
    x, y, z = u
    # Lorenz Mod1
    dxdt = -a*x+(y*y)-(z*z)+a*c
    dydt = x*(y-b*z)+d
    dzdt = z+x*(b*y+z)
    return(dxdt, dydt, dzdt)

# start values and initialization
#y0 = 0.05, 0.05, 0.05
y0 = 0.1, 0.1, 0.1
#y0 = 0.2, 0.2, 0.2
t = np.linspace(0, 10, 2000)
solution = odeint(calculate, y0, t, args = (a, b, c, d))
X, Y, Z = solution [:,0],   solution [:,1],   solution [:,2]
```

Robinson, C. (2000). Nonsymmetric Lorenz attractors from a homoclinic bifurcation. SIAM Journal on Mathematical Analysis, 32(1), 119-141, #26 LorenzMod1

```
import numpy as np
import matplotlib.pyplot as plt
from mpl_toolkits.mplot3d import Axes3D
from scipy.integrate import odeint

# Parameter
picname = "Lorenz_Mod2"
a = 0.9
b = 5
c = 9.9
d = 1
# basic equation
def calculate (u, t, a, b, c, d):
    x, y, z = u
    # Lorenz Mod2
    dxdt = -a*x+(y*y)-(z*z)+a*c
    dydt = x*(y-b*z)+d
    dzdt = z+x*(b*y+z)
    return(dxdt, dydt, dzdt)

# start values and initialization
y0 = 0.1, 0.1, 0.1
#t = np.linspace(0, 3, 2000)
t = np.linspace (0, 5, 2000)
solution = odeint(calculate , y0, t, args = (a, b, c, d))
X, Y, Z = solution [:,0], solution [:,1], solution [:,2]
```

XY

XZ

YZ

3d_Lorenz_Mod2

Kadir, A., Aili, M., Sattar, M. (2017). Color image encryption scheme using coupled hyper chaotic system with multiple impulse injections. Optik, 129, p.231-238, #27 LorenzMod2

```python
import numpy as np
import matplotlib.pyplot as plt
from mpl_toolkits.mplot3d import Axes3D
from scipy.integrate import odeint

# Parameter
picname = "Lorenz_Stenflow"
a = 2
b = 0.7
c = 26
d = 1.5
w = 0

# basic equation
def calculate (u, t, a, b, c, d,w):
    x, y, z = u
    # Lorenz Stenflow
    w = -x-a*w
    dxdt = a*(y-x)+d*w
    dydt = x*(c-z)-y
    dzdt = x*y-b*z
    return(dxdt, dydt, dzdt)

# start values and initialization
y0 = -1, 1, -1
t  = np.linspace(0, 30, 2000)
#t = np.linspace(0, 100, 4000)
solution = odeint(calculate , y0, t, args = (a, b, c, d,w))
X, Y, Z = solution [:,0],  solution [:,1],  solution [:,2]
```

XY

XZ

YZ

3d_Lorenz_Stenflow

UE Vincent. Synchronization of identical and non-identical 4-D chaotic systems using active control. In: Chaos, Solitons Fractals 37.4 (2008), p. 1065–1075, #28 Lorenz Stenflo
url: https://bit.ly/3oUgMl2 | url: https://doi.org/10.1016/j.chaos.2006.10.005

```python
import math
import numpy as np
import matplotlib. pyplot as plt
from mpl_toolkits. mplot3d import Axes3D
from scipy.integrate  import odeint

# Parameter
picname ="Lue-Chen"
a= -10
b= -4
c= 18.1

# basic equation
def calculate (u, t, a, b, c):
    x, y, z = u
    # Lue-Chen
    dxdt = -a*b*x/( a+b)-y*z+c
    dydt = a*y+x*z
    dzdt = b*z+x*y
    return(dxdt, dydt, dzdt)

# start values and initialization
y0 = 0, 0, 2
t  = np.linspace (0,  10,  2000)
solution  = odeint(calculate , y0, t, args = (a,b,c))
X, Y, Z = solution [:,0],  solution [:,1],  solution [:,2]
```

Lue, J., Chen, G., Zhang, S. (2002). The compound structure of a new chaotic attractor. Chaos, Solitons Fractals, 14(5), 669-672, #29 Lue-Chen

```python
import numpy as np
import matplotlib.pyplot as plt
from mpl_toolkits.mplot3d import Axes3D
from scipy.integrate import odeint

# Parameter
picname = "MooreSpiegel"
a = 100 # 150
b = 26 # 30, 40

# basic equation
def calculate (u, t, a, b):
    x, y, z = u
    # MooreSpiegel
    dxdt = y
    dydt = z
    dzdt = -z - (b - a + a*x*x)*y - b*x
    return(dxdt, dydt, dzdt)

# start values and initialization
y0 = -1.05, 0.9, 1.01
t = np.linspace (0, 10, 2000)
solution = odeint(calculate, y0, t, args = (a, b))
X, Y, Z = solution [:,0], solution [:,1], solution [:,2]
```

XY

XZ

YZ

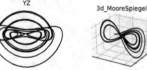
3d_MooreSpiegel

Leonard A Smith, C Ziehmann und K Fraedrich. Uncertainty dynamics and predictability in chaotic systems. In: Quarterly Journal of the Royal Meteorological Society 125.560 (1999), p. 2855–2886, #30 MooreSpiegel
url: https://doi.org/10.1002/qj.49712556005 | url: https://bit.ly/3ee0KxE

```python
import numpy as np
import math
import matplotlib. pyplot as plt
from mpl_toolkits. mplot3d import Axes3D
from scipy.integrate import odeint

# Parameter
picname = "MultiSprott_C"
a = 2.5
b = 1.5

# basic equation
def calculate (u, t, a, b):
    x, y, z = u
    # MultiSprott_C
    dxdt = a*(y-x)
    dydt = x*z
    dzdt = b-pow(y,2)
    return(dxdt, dydt, dzdt)

# start values and initialization
y0 = 0.1, 0.1, 0.1
t = np.linspace (0, 100, 2000)
solution = odeint(calculate , y0, t, args = (a, b))
X, Y, Z = solution [:,0], solution [:,1], solution [:,2]
```

Qiang Lai u. a. Dynamic analyses, FPGA implementation and engineering applications of multi-butterfly chaotic attractors generated from generalised Sprott C system. In: Pramana 90.1 (2018), p. 1–12, #31 MultiSprott C

```python
import numpy as np
import math
import matplotlib.pyplot as plt
from mpl_toolkits.mplot3d import Axes3D
from scipy.integrate import odeint

# Parameter
picname ="MuthuswamyChua"
a = 0.4
b = 1

# basic equation
def calculate (u, t, a, b):
    x, y, z = u
    # MuthuswamyChua
    dxdt = y
    dydt = -x/3 +y/2 -y*z*z/2
    dzdt = y -a*z -y*z
    return(dxdt, dydt, dzdt)

# start values and initialization
y0 = 0.1, 0.1, 0.1
t = np.linspace (0, 100, 2000)
solution = odeint(calculate , y0, t, args = (a, b))
X, Y, Z = solution [:,0], solution [:,1], solution [:,2]
```

Jaume Libre und Claudia Valls. On the integrability of a Muthuswamy-Chua system. In: Journal of Nonlinear Mathematical Physics 19.4 (2012), p. 477–488, #32 Muthuswamy-Chua
url: https://bit.ly/3svL4Lr

```python
import numpy as np
import math
import matplotlib.pyplot as plt
from mpl_toolkits.mplot3d import Axes3D
from scipy.integrate import odeint

# Parameter
picname ="NewtonLeipnik"
a = 0.4
b = 0.175

# basic equation
def calculate (u, t, a, b):
    x, y, z = u
    # NewtonLeipnik
    dxdt = -a*x+y+10*y*z
    dydt = -x-0.4*y+5*x*z
    dzdt = b*z-5*x*y
    return(dxdt, dydt, dzdt)

# start values and initialization
y0 = 0.349, 0, -0.16
t = np.linspace (0, 80, 2000)
solution = odeint(calculate , y0, t, args = (a, b))
X, Y, Z = solution [:,0], solution [:,1], solution [:,2]
```

XY   XZ

YZ   3d_NewtonLeipnik

Xuedi Wang und Chao Ge. Adaptive control and synchronization of the Newton-Leipnik systems. In: Journal of Information and Computing Science 3.4 (2008), p. 281289, #33 Newton-Leipnik
url: https://bit.ly/2Paj8PA

```python
import numpy as np
import math
import matplotlib. pyplot as plt
from mpl_toolkits. mplot3d import Axes3D
from scipy.integrate import odeint

# Parameter
picname ="NooseHover"
a = 1.5
b = 1

# basic equation
def calculate (u, t, a, b):
    x, y, z = u
    # Thomas
    dxdt = y
    dydt = -x + y*z
    dzdt = a - y*y
    return(dxdt, dydt, dzdt)

# start values and initialization
y0 = 1.0,  0,  0
t  = np.linspace (0,  50,  2000)
solution  = odeint(calculate ,  y0, t,  args = (a,  b))
X, Y,  Z = solution [:,0],    solution [:,1],    solution [:,2]
```

Shuichi Nos'e. A molecular dynamics method for simulations in the canonical ensemble. In: Molecular physics 52.2 (1984), p. 255–268, #34 Nose-Hoover

```python
import numpy as np
import matplotlib.pyplot as plt
from mpl_toolkits.mplot3d import Axes3D
from scipy.integrate import odeint

# Parameter
picname = "Qi-Chen"
a = 38      #36
b = 2.666
c = 80

# basic equation
def calculate (u, t, a, b, c):
    x, y, z = u
    # Qi-Chen
    dxdt = a*(y-x)+y*z
    dydt = c*x-y-x*z
    dzdt = x*y-b*z
    return(dxdt, dydt, dzdt)

# start values and initialization
y0 = 3.0, -4.0, 3.0
#y0 = -3, 2, 20
#y0 = -5, 5, 20
t = np.linspace (0, 3, 2000)
solution = odeint(calculate , y0, t, args = (a, b, c))
X, Y, Z = solution [:,0], solution [:,1], solution [:,2]
```

Sundarapandian Vaidyanathan. Adaptive controller and synchronizer design for the Qi-Chen chaotic system. In: International Conference on Computer Science and Information Technology. Springer 2012, p. 124–133, #35 Qi-Chen

```python
import numpy as np
import matplotlib.pyplot as plt
from mpl_toolkits.mplot3d import Axes3D
from scipy.integrate import odeint

# Parameter
picname = "RayleighBenard"
a = 9
r = 12
b = 5

# basic equation
def calculate (u, t, a, r, b):
    x, y, z = u
    # RayleighBenard
    dxdt = -a*x+a*y
    dydt = r*x-y-x*z
    dzdt = x*y-b*z
    return(dxdt, dydt, dzdt)

# start values and initialization
y0 = 0.1, 0.1, 0.1
t = np.linspace(0, 50, 4000)
solution = odeint(calculate , y0, t, args = (a, r, b))
X, Y, Z = solution [:,0],   solution [:,1],   solution [:,2]
```

Supriyo Paul u. a. Chaotic dynamics in two-dimensional Rayleigh-Benard convection. In: arXiv preprint arXiv:1005.5517 (2010), #36 Rayleigh Benard url: https://bit.ly/3cXzyUp

```python
import numpy as np
import matplotlib.pyplot as plt
from mpl_toolkits.mplot3d import Axes3D
from scipy.integrate import odeint

# Parameter
picname = "Rikitake "
a = 5
b = 2

# basic equation
def calculate (u, t, a, b):
    x, y, z = u
    # Rikitake
    dxdt = -b*x + z*y
    dydt = -b*y + (z - a)*x
    dzdt = 1.0 - x*y*y
    return(dxdt, dydt, dzdt)

# start values and initialization
y0 = 1.0, 1.0, 5.0
t = np.linspace(0, 40, 2000)
solution = odeint(calculate, y0, t, args = (a, b))
X, Y, Z = solution[:,0], solution[:,1], solution[:,2]
```

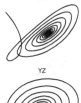

XY   XZ

YZ   3d_Rikitake

Tyler McMillen. The shape and dynamics of the Rikitake attractor. In: The Nonlinear Journal 1 (1999), p. 1–10, #37 Rikitake
url: https://bit.ly/3wz9DdD

```python
import numpy as np
import matplotlib. pyplot as plt
from mpl_toolkits. mplot3d import Axes3D
from scipy.integrate import odeint

# Parameter
picname = "Robinson"
a = 0.71
b = 1.8587
c = 0.7061
d = 0.1
v = 1

# basic equation
def calculate (u, t, a, b, c, d, v):
    x, y, z = u
    # Robinson
    dxdt = y
    dydt = x-2*pow(x,3)-a*y+b*x*x*y-v*y*z
    dzdt = -c*z + d*x*x
    return(dxdt, dydt, dzdt)

# start values and initialization
y0 = 0.1, 0.1, 0.1
t = np.linspace (0, 50, 2000)
solution = odeint(calculate , y0, t, args = (a, b, c, d, v))
X, Y, Z = solution [:,0], solution [:,1], solution [:,2]
```

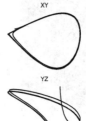
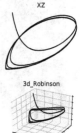

Paul Glendinning und Colin Sparrow. Shilnikov's saddlenode bifurcation. In: International Journal of Bifurcation and Chaos 6.06 (1996), p. 1153–1160, #38 Robinson
url: https://bit.ly/39XFlrk

```python
import numpy as np
import matplotlib. pyplot as plt
from mpl_toolkits. mplot3d import Axes3D
from scipy.integrate  import odeint

# Parameter
picname = "Roessler "
a = 0.2
b = 0.2
c = 5.7

# basic equation
def calculate ( u,  t,  a,  b,  c):
    x,  y,  z = u
    # Roessler
    dxdt = -(y + z)
    dydt = x +a*z
    dzdt = b + z*(x-c)
    return(dxdt,  dydt,  dzdt)

# start values and initialization
y0 = 6.0,   5.0,   1.0
t = np.linspace (0,   40,  2000)
solution  = odeint(calculate ,  y0,  t,  args = ( a,  b,  c))
X,  Y,  Z = solution [:,0],   solution [:,1],   solution [:,2]
```

O. E. Rössler, Continuous chaos: four prototype equations, Annals of the New York Academy of Sciences, 316, 376-392, 1979, #39 Roessler

```python
import numpy as np
import matplotlib. pyplot as plt
from mpl_toolkits. mplot3d import Axes3D
from scipy.integrate  import odeint

# Parameter
picname = "Rucklidge"
a = 6.7
k = 2

# basic equation
def calculate ( u,  t,  a,  k):
    x,  y,  z = u
    # Rucklidge
    dxdt = -k*x + a*y -y*z
    dydt = x
    dzdt = -z + y*y
    return(dxdt,  dydt,  dzdt)

# start values and initialization
y0 = 1.0,  0.0,  0.0
t  = np.linspace (0,  50,  2000)
#t = np.linspace(0, 100, 2000)
solution  = odeint(calculate ,  y0,  t,  args = (a,  k))
X,  Y,  Z = solution [:,0],    solution [:,1],    solution [:,2]
```

C.Ramanathan u. a. A new chaotic attractor from Rucklidge system and its application in secured communication using OFDM. In: 2017 11th International Conference on Intelligent Systems and Control (ISCO). IEEE. 2017, p. 241245, #40 Rucklidge url: https://doi.org/10.1109/ISCO.2017.7855989

```
import numpy as np
import matplotlib.pyplot as plt
from mpl_toolkits.mplot3d import Axes3D
from scipy.integrate import odeint

# Parameter
picname = "Sakarya"
a = 0.4
b = 0.3

# basic equation
def calculate (u, t, a, b):
    x, y, z = u
    # Sakarya
    dxdt = -x+y+(y*z)
    dydt = -x-y+a*(x*z)
    dzdt = z-b*(x*y)
    return(dxdt, dydt, dzdt)

# start values and initialization
y0 = 1, -1, 1
t = np.linspace (0, 40, 2000)
#t = np.linspace(0, 70, 4000)
solution = odeint(calculate , y0, t, args = (a, b))
X, Y, Z = solution [:,0],   solution [:,1],   solution [:,2]
```

XY

XZ

YZ

3d_Sakarya

Engin Can, Yilmaz Uyarouglu u. a. A new seven-term chaotic attractor and its hyperchaos. In: Optoelectronics and Advanced Materials-Rapid Communications 9.May-June 2015 (2015), p. 777–781, #41 Sakarya url: https://bit.ly/3dLulOO

```python
import numpy as np
import matplotlib. pyplot  as  plt
from mpl_toolkits. mplot3d import Axes3D
from scipy. integrate   import odeint

# Parameter
picname = "Shimizu-Morioka"
a = 0.75
b = 0.45

# basic equation
def calculate (u,  t,  a,  b):
    x,  y,  z = u
    # Shimizu-Morioka
    dxdt = y
    dydt = (1-z)*x-a*y
    dzdt = (x*x)-b*z
    return(dxdt,  dydt,  dzdt)

# start values and initialization
y0 = 0.1,  0.0,  0.0
#t = np.linspace(0,  30,  2000)
t = np.linspace (0,  100,  2000)
solution  = odeint(calculate ,  y0,  t,  args = (a,  b))
X,  Y,  Z = solution [:,0],   solution [:,1],   solution [:,2]
```

XY

XZ

YZ

3d_Shimizu-Morioka

Andrey L Shil'nikov. On bifurcations of the Lorenz attractor in the Shimizu-Morioka model. In: Physica D: Nonlinear Phenomena 62.1-4 (1993), p. 338–346, #42 Shimizu-Morioka
url: https://bit.ly/2Oys0yb

```
import numpy as np
import math
import matplotlib. pyplot as plt
from mpl_toolkits. mplot3d import Axes3D
from scipy.integrate  import odeint

# Parameter
picname = "SprottLinz_A"
a = 1
k = 1

# basic equation
def calculate (u, t, a, k):
    x, y, z = u
    # SprottLinz_A
    dxdt = y
    dydt = -x+y*z
    dzdt = 1-pow(y,2)
    return(dxdt, dydt, dzdt)

# start values and initialization
y0 = 0.1,  0.1,  0.1
t  = np.linspace (0,  50,  2000)
#t = np.linspace(0, 100, 2000)
solution  = odeint(calculate ,  y0, t,  args = (a,  k))
X, Y, Z = solution [:,0],   solution [:,1],   solution [:,2]
```

XY

XZ

YZ

3d_SprottLinz_A

Linz, Stefan J., and J. C. Sprott. Elementary chaotic flow. Physics Letters A 259.3-4 (1999): 240-245, #43 SprottLinz

```python
import numpy as np
import math
import matplotlib.pyplot as plt
from mpl_toolkits.mplot3d import Axes3D
from scipy.integrate  import odeint

# Parameter
picname = "SprottLinz_B"
a = 1
k = 1

# basic equation
def calculate (u, t, a, k):
    x, y, z = u
    # SprottLinz_B
    dxdt = y*z
    dydt = x-y
    dzdt = 1 -x*y
    return(dxdt, dydt, dzdt)

# start values and initialization
y0 = 1.0, 0.0, 0.0
t = np.linspace (0, 50, 2000)
#t = np.linspace(0, 100, 2000)
solution = odeint(calculate , y0, t, args = (a, k))
X, Y, Z = solution [:,0],   solution [:,1],   solution [:,2]
```

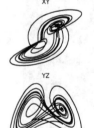

Linz, Stefan J., and J. C. Sprott. Elementary chaotic flow. Physics Letters A 259.3-4 (1999): 240-245, #44 SprottLinz

```python
import numpy as np
import math
import matplotlib.pyplot as plt
from mpl_toolkits.mplot3d import Axes3D
from scipy.integrate import odeint

# Parameter
picname = "SprottLinz_C"
a = 1
k = 1

# basic equation
def calculate (u, t, a, k):
    x, y, z = u
    # SprottLinz_C
    dxdt = y*z
    dydt = x - y
    dzdt = 1 -x*x
    return(dxdt, dydt, dzdt)

# start values and initialization
y0 = 1.0, 0.0, 1.0
t = np.linspace (0, 50, 2000)
#t = np.linspace(0, 100, 2000)
solution = odeint(calculate , y0, t, args = (a, k))
X, Y, Z = solution [:,0], solution [:,1], solution [:,2]
```

XY

XZ

YZ

3d_SprottLinz_C

Linz, Stefan J., and J. C. Sprott. Elementary chaotic flow. Physics Letters A 259.3-4 (1999): 240-245, #45 SprottLinz

```
import numpy as np
import math
import matplotlib. pyplot as plt
from mpl_toolkits. mplot3d import Axes3D
from scipy.integrate   import odeint

# Parameter
picname = "SprottLinz_D"
a = 3
k = 1

# basic equation
def calculate ( u,  t,  a,  k):
    x, y, z = u
    # SprottLinz_D
    dxdt = -y
    dydt = x+z
    dzdt = x*z+a*pow(y,2)
    return(dxdt,  dydt,  dzdt)

# start values and initialization
y0 = 0.1,   0.0,   0.0
t  = np.linspace (0,  50,  2000)
#t = np.linspace(0, 100, 2000)
solution  = odeint( calculate ,  y0,  t,  args  = ( a,  k))
X, Y, Z = solution [:,0],    solution [:,1],    solution [:,2]
```

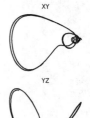

XY

XZ

YZ

3d_SprottLinz_D

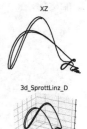

Linz, Stefan J., and J. C. Sprott. Elementary chaotic flow. Physics Letters A 259.3-4 (1999): 240-245, #46 SprottLinz

```python
import numpy as np
import math
import matplotlib.pyplot as plt
from mpl_toolkits.mplot3d import Axes3D
from scipy.integrate import odeint

# Parameter
picname = "SprottLinz_E"
a = 4
k = 1

# basic equation
def calculate (u, t, a, k):
    x, y, z = u
    # SprottLinz_E
    dxdt = y*z
    dydt = pow(x,2)-y
    dzdt = 1-a*x
    return(dxdt, dydt, dzdt)

# start values and initialization
y0 = 1.0, 0.0, 0.0
t = np.linspace (0, 50, 2000)
#t = np.linspace(0, 100, 2000)
solution = odeint(calculate , y0, t, args = (a, k))
X, Y, Z = solution [:,0], solution [:,1], solution [:,2]
```

XY

XZ

YZ

3d_SprottLinz_E

Linz, Stefan J., and J. C. Sprott. Elementary chaotic flow. Physics Letters A 259.3-4 (1999): 240-245, #47 SprottLinz

```python
import numpy as np
import math
import matplotlib. pyplot as plt
from mpl_toolkits. mplot3d import Axes3D
from scipy.integrate  import odeint

# Parameter
picname = "SprottLinz_F"
a = 0.5
k = 1

# basic equation
def calculate (u, t, a, k):
    x, y, z = u
    # SprottLinz_F
    dxdt = y+z
    dydt = -x+a*y
    dzdt = pow(x,2)-z
    return(dxdt, dydt, dzdt)

# start values and initialization
y0 = 0.1, 0.0, 0.0
t = np.linspace (0, 50, 2000)
#t = np.linspace(0, 100, 2000)
solution = odeint(calculate , y0, t, args = (a, k))
X, Y, Z = solution [:,0], solution [:,1], solution [:,2]
```

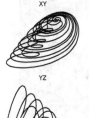

Linz, Stefan J., and J. C. Sprott. Elementary chaotic flow. Physics Letters A 259.3-4 (1999): 240-245, #48 SprottLinz

```python
import numpy as np
import math
import matplotlib.pyplot as plt
from mpl_toolkits.mplot3d import Axes3D
from scipy.integrate import odeint

# Parameter
picname = "SprottLinz_G"
a = 0.4
k = 1

# basic equation
def calculate (u, t, a, k):
    x, y, z = u
    # SprottLinz_G
    dxdt = a*x+z
    dydt = x*z-y
    dzdt = -x+y
    return(dxdt, dydt, dzdt)

# start values and initialization
y0 = 1.0, 0.0, 0.0
t = np.linspace (0, 50, 2000)
#t = np.linspace(0, 100, 2000)
solution = odeint(calculate , y0, t, args = (a, k))
X, Y, Z = solution [:,0], solution [:,1], solution [:,2]
```

Linz, Stefan J., and J. C. Sprott. Elementary chaotic flow. Physics Letters A 259.3-4 (1999): 240-245, #49 SprottLinz

```python
import numpy as np
import math
import matplotlib. pyplot as plt
from mpl_toolkits. mplot3d import Axes3D
from scipy.integrate import odeint

# Parameter
picname = "SprottLinz_H"
a = 0.5
k = 1

# basic equation
def calculate (u, t, a, k):
    x, y, z = u
    # SprottLinz_H
    dxdt = -y+pow(z,2)
    dydt = x+a*y
    dzdt = x-z
    return(dxdt, dydt, dzdt)

# start values and initialization
y0 = 1.0, 0.0, 0.0
t = np.linspace (0, 50, 2000)
#t = np.linspace(0, 100, 2000)
solution = odeint(calculate , y0, t, args = (a, k))
X, Y, Z = solution [:,0], solution [:,1], solution [:,2]
```

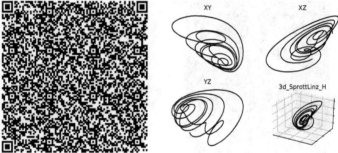

Linz, Stefan J., and J. C. Sprott. Elementary chaotic flow. Physics Letters A 259.3-4 (1999): 240-245, #50 SprottLinz

```python
import numpy as np
import math
import matplotlib.pyplot as plt
from mpl_toolkits.mplot3d import Axes3D
from scipy.integrate import odeint

# Parameter
picname = "SprottLinz_I "
a = -0.2
k = 1

# basic equation
def calculate (u, t, a, k):
    x, y, z = u
    # SprottLinz_I
    dxdt = a*y
    dydt = x+z
    dzdt = x+pow(y,2)-z
    return(dxdt, dydt, dzdt)

# start values and initialization
y0 = 0.1, 0.1, 0.1
t = np.linspace (0, 50, 2000)
#t = np.linspace(0, 100, 2000)
solution = odeint(calculate , y0, t, args = (a, k))
X, Y, Z = solution [:,0], solution [:,1], solution [:,2]
```

Linz, Stefan J., and J. C. Sprott. Elementary chaotic flow. Physics Letters A 259.3-4 (1999): 240-245, #51 SprottLinz

```python
import numpy as np
import math
import matplotlib. pyplot as plt
from mpl_toolkits. mplot3d import Axes3D
from scipy.integrate import odeint

# Parameter
picname = "SprottLinz_J"
a = 2
k = 1

# basic equation
def calculate (u, t, a, k):
    x, y, z = u
    # SprottLinz_J
    dxdt = a*z
    dydt = -a*y + z
    dzdt = -x + y + y*y
    return(dxdt, dydt, dzdt)

# start values and initialization
y0 = 0.1,  0.0,  0.0
t  = np.linspace (0,  50,  2000)
#t = np.linspace(0, 100, 2000)
solution  = odeint(calculate , y0, t, args = (a, k))
X, Y, Z = solution [:,0],  solution [:,1],  solution [:,2]
```

Linz, Stefan J., and J. C. Sprott. Elementary chaotic flow. Physics Letters A 259.3-4 (1999): 240-245, #52 SprottLinz

```python
import numpy as np
import math
import matplotlib.pyplot as plt
from mpl_toolkits.mplot3d import Axes3D
from scipy.integrate import odeint

# Parameter
picname = "SprottLinz_K"
a = 0.3
k = 1

# basic equation
def calculate (u, t, a, k):
    x, y, z = u
    # SprottLinz_K
    dxdt = x*y-z
    dydt = x-y
    dzdt = x+a*z
    return(dxdt, dydt, dzdt)

# start values and initialization
y0 = 0.1, 0.0, 0.0
t = np.linspace (0, 50, 2000)
#t = np.linspace(0, 100, 2000)
solution = odeint(calculate , y0, t, args = (a, k))
X, Y, Z = solution [:,0], solution [:,1], solution [:,2]
```

XY   XZ

YZ   3d_SprottLinz_K

Linz, Stefan J., and J. C. Sprott. Elementary chaotic flow. Physics Letters A 259.3-4 (1999): 240-245, #53 SprottLinz

```python
import numpy as np
import math
import matplotlib.pyplot as plt
from mpl_toolkits.mplot3d import Axes3D
from scipy.integrate import odeint

# Parameter
picname = "SprottLinz_L"
a = 3.9
b = 0.9

# basic equation
def calculate (u, t, a, b):
    x, y, z = u
    # SprottLinz_L
    dxdt = y+a*z
    dydt = b*pow(x,2)-y
    dzdt = 1-x
    return(dxdt, dydt, dzdt)

# start values and initialization
y0 = 1.0, 0.0, 0.0
t = np.linspace (0, 50, 2000)
#t = np.linspace(0, 100, 2000)
solution = odeint(calculate , y0, t, args = (a, b))
X, Y, Z = solution [:,0], solution [:,1], solution [:,2]
```

Linz, Stefan J., and J. C. Sprott. Elementary chaotic flow. Physics Letters A 259.3-4 (1999): 240-245, #54 SprottLinz

```python
import numpy as np
import math
import matplotlib.pyplot as plt
from mpl_toolkits.mplot3d import Axes3D
from scipy.integrate import odeint

# Parameter
picname = "SprottLinz_M"
a = 1.7
k = 1

# basic equation
def calculate (u, t, a, k):
    x, y, z = u
    # SprottLinz_M
    dxdt = -z
    dydt = -x*x -y
    dzdt = a + a*x + y
    return(dxdt, dydt, dzdt)

# start values and initialization
y0 = 0.1, 0.0, 0.0
t = np.linspace (0, 50, 2000)
#t = np.linspace(0, 100, 2000)
solution = odeint(calculate , y0, t, args = (a, k))
X, Y, Z = solution [:,0], solution [:,1], solution [:,2]
```

Linz, Stefan J., and J. C. Sprott. Elementary chaotic flow. Physics Letters A 259.3-4 (1999): 240-245, #55 SprottLinz

```
import numpy as np
import math
import matplotlib. pyplot as plt
from mpl_toolkits. mplot3d import Axes3D
from scipy.integrate   import odeint

# Parameter
picname = "SprottLinz_N"
a = 2
k = 1

# basic equation
def calculate (u, t, a, k):
    x, y, z = u
    # SprottLinz_N
    dxdt = -a*y
    dydt = x + pow(z,2)
    dzdt = 1+y-a*z
    return(dxdt, dydt, dzdt)

# start values and initialization
y0 = 0.1,  0.0,  0.0
t  = np.linspace (0,  50,  2000)
#t = np.linspace(0, 100, 2000)
solution = odeint(calculate , y0, t, args = (a, k))
X, Y, Z = solution [:,0],    solution [:,1],    solution [:,2]
```

XY

XZ

YZ

3d_SprottLinz_N

Linz, Stefan J., and J. C. Sprott. Elementary chaotic flow. Physics Letters A 259.3-4 (1999): 240-245, #56 SprottLinz

```
import numpy as np
import math
import matplotlib.pyplot as plt
from mpl_toolkits.mplot3d import Axes3D
from scipy.integrate import odeint

# Parameter
picname = "SprottLinz_O"
a = 2.7
k = 1

# basic equation
def calculate (u, t, a, k):
    x, y, z = u
    # SprottLinz_O
    dxdt = y
    dydt = x-z
    dzdt = x+x*z+a*y
    return(dxdt, dydt, dzdt)

# start values and initialization
y0 = 0.1, 0.1, 0.1
t = np.linspace(0, 50, 2000)
#t = np.linspace(0, 100, 2000)
solution = odeint(calculate , y0, t, args = (a, k))
X, Y, Z = solution [:,0],   solution [:,1],   solution [:,2]
```

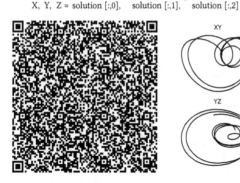
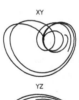

Linz, Stefan J., and J. C. Sprott. Elementary chaotic flow. Physics Letters A 259.3-4 (1999): 240-245, #57 SprottLinz

```python
import numpy as np
import math
import matplotlib.pyplot as plt
from mpl_toolkits.mplot3d import Axes3D
from scipy.integrate import odeint

# Parameter
picname = "SprottLinz_P"
a = 2.7
k = 1

# basic equation
def calculate (u, t, a, k):
    x, y, z = u
    # SprottLinz_P
    dxdt = a*y+z
    dydt = -x + pow(y,2)
    dzdt = x+y
    return(dxdt, dydt, dzdt)

# start values and initialization
y0 = 0.1, 0.1, 0.1
t = np.linspace (0, 50, 2000)
#t = np.linspace(0, 100, 2000)
solution = odeint(calculate , y0, t, args = (a, k))
X, Y, Z = solution [:,0], solution [:,1], solution [:,2]
```

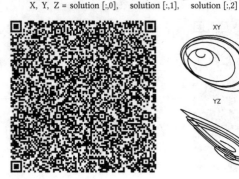

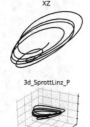

Linz, Stefan J., and J. C. Sprott. Elementary chaotic flow. Physics Letters A 259.3-4 (1999): 240-245, #58 SprottLinz

```python
import numpy as np
import math
import matplotlib. pyplot as plt
from mpl_toolkits. mplot3d import Axes3D
from scipy.integrate import odeint

# Parameter
picname = "SprottLinz_Q"
a = 3.4
b = 0.5

# basic equation
def calculate (u, t, a, b):
    x, y, z = u
    # SprottLinz_Q
    dxdt = -z
    dydt = x-y
    dzdt = a*x + math.pow(y,2) + b*z
    return(dxdt, dydt, dzdt)

# start values and initialization
y0 = 0.1, 0.1, 0.1
t = np.linspace (0, 50, 2000)
#t = np.linspace(0, 100, 2000)
solution = odeint(calculate , y0, t, args = (a, b))
X, Y, Z = solution [:,0], solution [:,1], solution [:,2]
```

XY

XZ

YZ

3d_SprottLinz_Q

Linz, Stefan J., and J. C. Sprott. Elementary chaotic flow. Physics Letters A 259.3-4 (1999): 240-245, #59 SprottLinz

```python
import numpy as np
import math
import matplotlib.pyplot as plt
from mpl_toolkits.mplot3d import Axes3D
from scipy.integrate import odeint

# Parameter
picname = "SprottLinz_R"
a = 0.9
b = 0.4

# basic equation
def calculate (u, t, a, b):
    x, y, z = u
    # SprottLinz_R
    dxdt = a - y
    dydt = b + z
    dzdt = x*y - z
    return(dxdt, dydt, dzdt)

# start values and initialization
y0 = 0.1, 0.0, 0.0
t = np.linspace (0, 50, 2000)
#t = np.linspace(0, 100, 2000)
solution = odeint(calculate , y0, t, args = (a, b))
X, Y, Z = solution [:,0], solution [:,1], solution [:,2]
```

Linz, Stefan J., and J. C. Sprott. Elementary chaotic flow. Physics Letters A 259.3-4 (1999): 240-245, #60 SprottLinz

```python
import numpy as np
import math
import matplotlib.pyplot as plt
from mpl_toolkits.mplot3d import Axes3D
from scipy.integrate import odeint

# Parameter
picname = "SprottLinz_S"
a = 4
k = 1

# basic equation
def calculate (u, t, a, k):
    x, y, z = u
    # SprottLinz_S
    dxdt = -x-a*y
    dydt = x+ math.pow(z,2)
    dzdt = 1+x
    return(dxdt, dydt, dzdt)

# start values and initialization
y0 = 1.0,  0.0,  0.0
t  = np.linspace (0,  30,  2000)
#t = np.linspace(0, 100, 2000)
solution  = odeint(calculate ,  y0, t,  args = (a, k))
X, Y, Z = solution [:,0],   solution [:,1],   solution [:,2]
```

XY

XZ

YZ

3d_SprottLinz_S

Linz, Stefan J., and J. C. Sprott. Elementary chaotic flow. Physics Letters A 259.3-4 (1999): 240-245, #61 SprottLinz

```python
import math
import numpy as np
import matplotlib.pyplot as plt
from mpl_toolkits.mplot3d import Axes3D
from scipy.integrate import odeint

# Parameter
picname ="Tamari"
a= 1.013
b= -0.011
c= 0.02
d= 0.96
e= 0.0
f= 0.01
g= 1.0
h= 0.05
i= 0.05

# basic equation
def calculate (u, t, a, b,c,d,e,f,g,h,i):
    x, y, z = u
    # Tamari
    dxdt= (x-a*y)*np.cos(z)-b*y*np.sin(z);
    dydt= (x+c*y)*np.sin(z)+d*y*np.cos(z);
    dzdt= e+f*z+g*math.atan((1-i)*y/(1-h)*x);
    return(dxdt, dydt, dzdt)

# start values and initialization
y0 = 1, 1, 1
t = np.linspace(0, 140, 2000)
solution = odeint(calculate, y0, t, args = (a, b,c,d,e,f,g,h,i))
X, Y, Z = solution[:,0], solution[:,1], solution[:,2]
```

Tamari, Ben. Conservation and Symmetry Laws and Stabilization Programs in Economics. Ecometry, 1997, #62 Tamari

```python
import numpy as np
import matplotlib.pyplot as plt
from mpl_toolkits.mplot3d import Axes3D
from scipy.integrate import odeint

# Parameter
picname ="Thomas"
a = 1
b = 0.19

# basic equation
def calculate (u, t, a, b):
    x, y, z = u
    # Thomas
    dxdt = -b*x + np.sin(y)
    dydt = -b*y + np.sin(z)
    dzdt = -b*z + np.sin(x)
    return(dxdt, dydt, dzdt)

# start values and initialization
y0 = -1.0, 0.9, 1.0
t = np.linspace(0, 340, 2000)
solution = odeint(calculate, y0, t, args = (a, b))
X, Y, Z = solution [:,0], solution [:,1], solution [:,2]
```

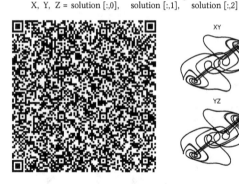
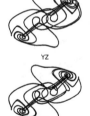
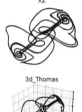

Rhode, M. A., Rollins, R. W., Markworth, A. J., Edwards, K. D., Nguyen, K., Daw, C. S., Thomas, J. F. (1995). Controlling chaos in a model of thermal pulse combustion. Journal of Applied Physics, 78(4), 2224-2232, #63 Thomas

```python
import numpy as np
import matplotlib. pyplot as plt
from mpl_toolkits. mplot3d import Axes3D
from scipy.integrate   import odeint

# Parameter
picname ="Tsucs1"
a = 40
c = 0.833
d = 0.5
e = 0.65
f = 20

# basic equation
def calculate (u, t, a,c,d,e,f):
    x, y, z = u
    # Tsucs1
    dxdt = a*(y-x)+d*x*z
    dydt = f*y-x*z
    dzdt = c*z+x*y-e*x*x
    return(dxdt, dydt, dzdt)

# start values and initialization
y0 = 0.1, 1.0, -0.1
t = np.linspace (0, 5, 2000)
#t = np.linspace(0, 15, 8000)
solution = odeint(calculate , y0, t, args = (a,c,d,e,f))
X, Y, Z = solution [:,0], solution [:,1], solution [:,2]
```

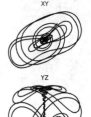

Lin Pan u. a. A new three-scroll unified chaotic system coined. In: International Journal of Nonlinear Science 10.4 (2010), p. 462–474, #64 TSUCS 1 url: https://bit.ly/2Q9XLyp

```python
import numpy as np
import matplotlib.pyplot as plt
from mpl_toolkits.mplot3d import Axes3D
from scipy.integrate import odeint

# Parameter
picname ="Wang"
a = 0.977
b = 10
c = 4
d = 0.1

# basic equation
def calculate (u, t, a, b, c, d):
    x, y, z = u
    # Wang
    dxdt = a*(x-y)-y*z
    dydt = -b*y+x*z
    dzdt = -c*z+d*x+x*y
    return(dxdt, dydt, dzdt)

# start values and initialization
y0 = 0.1, 0.1, 0.1
t = np.linspace (0, 20, 2000)
#t = np.linspace(0, 100, 4000)
solution = odeint(calculate , y0, t, args = (a, b, c, d))
X, Y, Z = solution [:,0], solution [:,1], solution [:,2]
```

Zenghui Wang u. a. A 3-D four-wing attractor and its analysis. In: Brazilian Journal of Physics 39.3 (2009), p. 547–553, #65 Wang
url: https://bit.ly/3ejePtJ

```python
import numpy as np
import matplotlib.pyplot as plt
from mpl_toolkits.mplot3d import Axes3D
from scipy.integrate import odeint

# Parameter
picname ="WangSun"
a = 0.2
b = -0.01
c = 1
d = -0.4
e = -1.0
f = -1.0

# basic equation
def calculate (u, t, a, b, c, d, e, f):
    x, y, z = u
    # Wang
    dxdt = a*x + c*y*z
    dydt = b*x + d*y-x*z
    dzdt = e*z + f*x*y
    return(dxdt, dydt, dzdt)

# start values and initialization
y0 = 0.3, 0.1, 1
t = np.linspace (0, 200, 4000)
solution = odeint(calculate , y0, t, args = (a, b, c, d, e, f))
X, Y, Z = solution [:,0], solution [:,1], solution [:,2]
```

XY

XZ

YZ

3d_WangSun

Wang, Z., Sun, W., Wei, Z., Zhang, S. (2015). Dynamics and delayed feedback control for a 3D jerk system with hidden attractor.
Nonlinear Dynamics, 82(1), p. 577-588, #66 Wang-Sun

```python
import math
import numpy as np
import matplotlib.pyplot as plt
from mpl_toolkits.mplot3d import Axes3D
from scipy.integrate import odeint

# Parameter
picname ="WimolBanlue"
a = 0.2
b = -0.01

# basic equation
def calculate (u, t, a, b):
    x, y, z = u
    # WimolBanlue
    dxdt = y-x
    dydt = -z* np.tanh(x)
    dzdt = -a+x*y+abs(y)
    return(dxdt, dydt, dzdt)

# start values and initialization
y0 = 1, 1, 1
t = np.linspace(0, 200, 4000)
solution = odeint(calculate , y0, t, args = (a, b))
X, Y, Z = solution [:,0], solution [:,1], solution [:,2]
```

XY   XZ

YZ   3d_WimolBanlue

Wimol San-Um und Banlue Srisuchinwong. Highly Complex Chaotic System with Piecewise Linear Nonlinearity and Compound Structures. In: Journal of Computers 7.4 (2012), p. 1041–1047, #67 Wimol-Banlue
url: https://bit.ly/3JRQZDI

```python
import numpy as np
import matplotlib.pyplot as plt
from mpl_toolkits.mplot3d import Axes3D
from scipy.integrate import odeint

# Parameter
picname = "XingYun"
a = 50
b = 10
c = 13
e = 6

# basic equation
def calculate (u, t, a, b, c, e):
    x, y, z = u
    # XingYun
    dxdt = a*(y-x) + y*z*z
    dydt = b*(x + y) - x*z*z
    dzdt = -c*z + e*y + x*y*z
    return(dxdt, dydt, dzdt)

# start values and initialization
y0 = 3, 3, 0.1
t = np.linspace(0, 3, 4000)
solution = odeint(calculate , y0, t, args = (a, b, c, e))
X, Y, Z = solution [:,0],  solution [:,1],  solution [:,2]
```

Liu Xing-Yun. A new 3D four-wing chaotic system with cubic nonlinearity and its circuit implementation. In: Chinese Physics Letters 26.9 (2009), p. 090504, #68 Xing-Yun

```
import numpy as np
import matplotlib.pyplot as plt
from mpl_toolkits.mplot3d import Axes3D
from scipy.integrate import odeint

# Parameter
picname ="YangCao"
a = 2.97
b = 0.15
c = -3
d = 1
e = -8.78

# basic equation
def calculate (u, t, a, b, c, d, e):
    x, y, z = u
    # XingYun
    dxdt = a*x + b*y + y*z
    dydt = c*y -x*z + d*y*z
    dzdt = e*z -x*y
    return(dxdt, dydt, dzdt)

# start values and initialization
y0 = 3, 1, 1
t = np.linspace (0, 13, 4000)
solution = odeint(calculate , y0, t, args = (a, b, c, d, e))
X, Y, Z = solution [:,0], solution [:,1], solution [:,2]
```

XY

YZ

XZ

3d_YangCao

Yang Cao. A new hybrid chaotic map and its application on image encryption and hiding. In: Mathematical Problems in Engineering 2013 (2013), #69 Yang Cao url: https://doi.org/10.1155/2013/728375

```python
import math
import numpy as np
import matplotlib. pyplot as plt
from mpl_toolkits. mplot3d import Axes3D
from scipy.integrate  import odeint

# Parameter
picname ="YuWang"
a = 10
b = 40
c = 2
d = 2.5

# basic equation
def calculate ( u,  t, a, b, c, d):
    x,  y,  z = u
    # YuWang
    dxdt = a*(y-x)
    dydt = b*x - c*x*z
    dzdt = math.exp(x*y) -d*z
    return(dxdt,  dydt,  dzdt)

# start values and initialization
y0 = 2.2,  2.4,  28
t  = np.linspace (0,  7,  4000)
solution  = odeint(calculate ,  y0,  t,  args = (a, b, c, d))
X, Y, Z = solution [:,0],   solution [:,1],   solution [:,2]
```

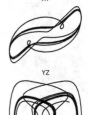

XY

YZ

XZ

3d_YuWang

Fei Yu und Chunhua Wang. A novel three dimension autonomous chaotic system with a quadratic exponential nonlinear term. In: Engineering, Technology Applied Science Research 2.2 (2012), p. 209–215, #70 Yu-Wang

```python
import numpy as np
import matplotlib. pyplot as plt
from mpl_toolkits. mplot3d import Axes3D
from scipy.integrate  import odeint

# Parameter
picname ="Zhou"
a = 10
b = 16
c = -1

# basic equation
def calculate (u,  t, a, b, c):
    x, y, z = u
    # Zhou
    dxdt = a*(y - x)
    dydt = b*x - x*z
    dzdt = x*y + c*z
    return(dxdt, dydt, dzdt)

# start values and initialization
y0 = 3, 1,  15
t = np.linspace (0,  10,  4000)
solution  = odeint(calculate ,  y0, t,  args = (a, b, c))
X, Y, Z = solution [:,0],   solution [:,1],   solution [:,2]
```

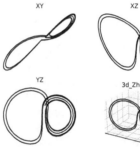

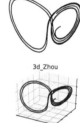

Ummu Atiqah Mohd Roslan, Zabidin Salleh und A Kiliccman. Solving Zhou Chaotic System Using Fourth-Order Runge-Kutta Method. In: World Applied Sciences Journal 21.6 (2013), p. 939–944, #71 Zhou

```python
import numpy as np
import matplotlib. pyplot  as  plt
from mpl_toolkits. mplot3d import Axes3D
from scipy.integrate   import odeint

# Parameter
picname ="ZhouChen"
a = 2.97
b = 0.15
c = -3
d = 1
e = -8.78

# basic equation
def calculate (u,  t, a, b, c, d, e):
    x,  y,  z = u
    # ZhouChen
    dxdt = a*x + b*y + y*z
    dydt = c*y - x*z + d*y*z
    dzdt = e*z - x*y
    return(dxdt,  dydt,  dzdt)

# start values and initialization
y0 = 3,  1,  1
t  = np.linspace (0,   10,  4000)
solution  = odeint(calculate ,  y0,  t,  args  = (a, b, c, d, e))
X,  Y,  Z = solution [:,0],    solution [:,1],    solution [:,2]
```

Yang, Q., Chen, G., Zhou, T. (2006). A unified Lorenz-type system and its canonical form. International Journal of Bifurcation and Chaos, 16(10), 2855-2871, #72 ZhouChen

```python
import numpy as np
import matplotlib.pyplot as plt
from mpl_toolkits.mplot3d import Axes3D
from scipy.integrate import odeint

# Parameter
picname ="ElhadjSprottAttraktor "
a =  40
b =  33
c =  10

# basic equation
def calculate (u, t, a, b, c):
    x, y, z = u
    # ElhadjSprottAttraktor
    dxdt = a*(y-x)
    dydt = -a*x-b*y*z
    dzdt = -c+y*y
    return(dxdt, dydt, dzdt)

# start values and initialization
y0 = 0.1,  0.2,  0.1
t  = np.linspace (0,  3,  2000)
#t = np.linspace(0, 30, 2000)
#t = np.linspace(0, 100, 2000)
solution = odeint(calculate , y0, t, args = (a, b, c))
X, Y, Z = solution [:,0],  solution [:,1],  solution [:,2]
```

XY

XZ

YZ

3d_ElhadjSprottAttraktor

Elhadj, Z., Sprott, J. C. (2008). On the robustness of chaos in dynamical systems: Theories and applications. Frontiers of Physics in China, 3(2), 195, #73 ElhadjSprott

```python
import numpy as np
import matplotlib.pyplot as plt
from mpl_toolkits.mplot3d import Axes3D
from scipy.integrate import odeint

# Parameter
picname = "LotkeVoltera"
a = 2.9851
b = 3
c = 2

# basic equation
def calculate (u, t, a, b, c):
    x, y, z = u
    # LotkeVoltera
    dxdt = x - x*y + c*x*x - a*z*x*x
    dydt = -y + x*y
    dzdt = -b*z + a*z*x*x
    return(dxdt, dydt, dzdt)

# start values and initialization
y0 = 2.0, 2.0, 2.0
t = np.linspace (0, 10, 2000)
solution = odeint(calculate, y0, t, args = (a, b, c))
X, Y, Z = solution [:,0], solution [:,1], solution [:,2]
```

Hou, Z. (1999). Global attractor in autonomous competitive Lotka-Volterra systems. Proceedings of the American Mathematical Society, 127(12), 3633-3642, #74 Lotke-Voltera

```python
import numpy as np
import matplotlib.pyplot as plt
from mpl_toolkits.mplot3d import Axes3D
from scipy.integrate import odeint

# Parameter
picname = "RabinovichFabrikant"
a = 0.14   # a= 1.1,  0.98
b = 0.1    # b= 0.87, 0.14

# basic equation
def calculate (u, t, a, b):
    x, y, z = u
    # RabinovichFabrikant
    dxdt = y*(z - 1 + x*x) + b*x
    dydt = x*(3*z + 1 -x*x) + b*y
    dzdt = -2*z*(a + x*y)
    return(dxdt, dydt, dzdt)

# start values and initialization
y0 = -1.05,  0.9,  1.01
t = np.linspace (0,  30,  2000)
solution = odeint(calculate , y0, t, args = (a, b))
X, Y, Z = solution [:,0],   solution [:,1],   solution [:,2]
```

XY   XZ

YZ   3d_RabinovichFabrikant

Danca, M. F., Bourke, P., Kuznetsov, N. (2019). Graphical structure of attraction basins of hidden chaotic attractors: The Rabinovich–Fabrikant system. International Journal of Bifurcation and Chaos, 29(01), 1930001, #75 RabinovichFabrikant

```python
import numpy as np
import matplotlib.pyplot as plt
from mpl_toolkits.mplot3d import Axes3D
from scipy.integrate import odeint

# Parameter
picname = "offset1 "
a = 2.2
b = 0.7

# basic equation
def calculate (u, t, a, b):
    x, y, z = u
    # offset1
    dxdt = 1 - a*y*z
    dydt = z*z - z
    dzdt = x - b*z
    return(dxdt, dydt, dzdt)

# start values and initialization
#y0 = 0.1,0.1,0.1
#y0 = 0.5,0.5,0.5
y0 = 1.9,1.9,1.9
t = np.linspace (0, 50, 2000)
solution = odeint(calculate , y0, t, args = (a, b))
X, Y, Z = solution [:,0], solution [:,1], solution [:,2]
```

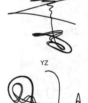

Li, C., Jiang, Y., and Ma, X.
On offset boosting in chaotic system.
Chaos Theory and Applications, 3(2), 47-54, 2021, #76 offset1

```python
import numpy as np
import matplotlib. pyplot as plt
from mpl_toolkits. mplot3d import Axes3D
from scipy.integrate import odeint

# Parameter
picname = "offset2 "
a = 2.2
b = 0.7

# basic equation
def calculate (u, t, a, b):
    x, y, z = u
    # offset2
    dxdt = 1 - 2*a*np.cos(y)*z
    dydt = z*z - z
    dzdt = x - b*z
    return(dxdt, dydt, dzdt)

# start values and initialization
#y0 = 0.1,0.1,0.1
#y0 = 0.5,0.5,0.5
y0 = 1.0,1.0,1.0
t = np.linspace (0, 50, 2000)
solution = odeint(calculate , y0, t, args = (a, b))
X, Y, Z = solution [:,0],  solution [:,1],  solution [:,2]
```

XY

XZ

YZ

3d_offset2

Li, C., Jiang, Y., and Ma, X.
On offset boosting in chaotic system.
Chaos Theory and Applications, 3(2), 47-54, 2021, #77 offset2

```python
import math
import numpy as np
import matplotlib.pyplot as plt
from mpl_toolkits.mplot3d import Axes3D
from scipy.integrate import odeint

# Parameter
picname = "offset3 "
a = 3.55
b = 0.6
c = 0

# basic equation
def calculate (u, t, a, b):
    x, y, z = u
    # offset3
    dxdt = 1 - a*(abs(y))*z
    dydt = np.sign(y)*(z*z - z)
    dzdt = 3*math.sin(x) - b*z
    return(dxdt, dydt, dzdt)

# start values and initialization
#y0 = 0.5,0.5,0.5
y0 = 1.0,1.0,1.0
t = np.linspace(0, 20, 2000)
solution = odeint(calculate , y0, t, args = (a, b))
X, Y, Z = solution [:,0], solution [:,1], solution [:,2]
```

XY

XZ

YZ

3d_offset3

Li, C., Jiang, Y., and Ma, X.
On offset boosting in chaotic system.
Chaos Theory and Applications, 3(2), 47-54, 2021, #78 offset3

```python
import math
import numpy as np
import matplotlib.pyplot as plt
from mpl_toolkits.mplot3d import Axes3D
from scipy.integrate import odeint

# Parameter
picname = "offset4 "
a = 5
b = 1

# basic equation
def calculate (u, t, a, b):
    x, y, z = u
    # offset4
    dxdt = y
    dydt = -x-np.sign(z)*y
    dzdt = y*y - math.exp(-x*x)
    return(dxdt, dydt, dzdt)

# start values and initialization
#y0 = 0.1,0.1,0.1
#y0 = 0.5,0.5,0.5
y0 = 1.4,1.9,-3.9
t = np.linspace(0, 100, 2000)
solution = odeint(calculate , y0, t, args = (a, b))
X, Y, Z = solution [:,0], solution [:,1], solution [:,2]
```

Li, C., Jiang, Y., and Ma, X.
On offset boosting in chaotic system.
Chaos Theory and Applications, 3(2), 47-54, 2021, #79 offset4

```
import numpy as np
import matplotlib.pyplot as plt
from mpl_toolkits.mplot3d import Axes3D
from scipy.integrate import odeint

# Parameter
picname = "RK5_Butcher"
a = 5
b = 1

# basic equation
def calculate (u, t, a, b):
    x, y, z = u
    # Tuna
    dxdt = y*(1-z)
    dydt = y*(1 + z) -a*x
    dzdt = a -x*y -y*y
    return(dxdt, dydt, dzdt)

# start values and initialization
#y0 = -3.9, 0.9, -4.1
#y0 = -4.3, 0.9, -4.1
y0 = -4.9, 0.9, -4.1
#y0 = -5.9, 0.9, -4.1
t = np.linspace (0, 20, 2000)
solution = odeint(calculate , y0, t, args = (a, b))
X, Y, Z = solution [:,0], solution [:,1], solution [:,2]
```

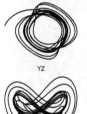
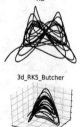

Alcin, M., Tuna, M., Erdogmus, P. and Koyuncu,
I. FPGA-based Dual Core TRNG Design Using Ring and Runge-Kutta-Butcher
based on Chaotic Oscillator. Chaos Theory and Applications, 3(1), 20-28, 2021, #80
RK5Butcher

```python
import numpy as np
import matplotlib.pyplot as plt
from mpl_toolkits.mplot3d import Axes3D
from scipy.integrate import odeint

# Parameter
picname = "Pickover"
a = 2.24
b = 0.43
c = -0.65    # -2.65
d = -2.43

# basic equation
def calculate (u, t, a, b, c, d):
    x, y, z = u
    # Pickover
    dxdt = np.sin(a*y) - z*np.cos(b*x)
    dydt = z * np.sin(c*x) - np.cos(d*x)
    dzdt = x * np.sin(a)
    return(dxdt, dydt, dzdt)

# start values and initialization
#y0 = 1.0, 1.0, 1.0
#y0 = 0.5, 0.5, 0.5
y0 = 0.1, 0.1, 0.1
t = np.linspace(0, 25, 2000)
solution = odeint(calculate , y0, t, args = (a, b, c, d))
X, Y, Z = solution [:,0],    solution [:,1],    solution [:,2]
```

XY

XZ

YZ

3d_Pickover

Pickover, C. A. Attractors With Dueling Symmetry. Chaos and Fractals: A Computer Graphical Journey, 1998, p. 61,#81 Pickover

```python
import numpy as np
import matplotlib.pyplot as plt
from mpl_toolkits.mplot3d import Axes3D
from scipy.integrate import odeint

# Parameter
picname = "Lorenz_M4"
a = 0.9
b = 0.1
c = 14
k = 2.5
g = 0

# basic equation
def calculate (u, t, a, b, c,k, g):
    x, y, z = u
    # Lorenz M4
    short = np.sign(x-4.1) -np.sign(x+5.1)
    g = 1.1165*(2 + short)
    #g = 1.1165*2
    dxdt = a*(y -x)
    dydt = -z*np.sign(x)
    dzdt = g - 1
    return(dxdt, dydt, dzdt)

# start values and initialization
y0 = 1, 1, 1
t = np.linspace (0, 100, 2000)
solution = odeint(calculate , y0, t, args = (a, b, c,k, g))
X, Y, Z = solution [:,0], solution [:,1], solution [:,2]
```

XY

XZ

YZ

3d_Lorenz_M4

Ghys, É. (2013, October). The Lorenz attractor, a paradigm for chaos. In Chaos: Poincaré Seminar 2010 (pp. 1-54). Basel: Springer Basel

```python
import math
import numpy as np
import matplotlib.pyplot as plt
from mpl_toolkits.mplot3d import Axes3D
from scipy.integrate import odeint

picname ="3-layer"                # Parameter
a1 = -4.1
a2 = 1.2
a3 = 13.45
c1 = 2.76
c2 = 0.6
c3 = 13.13
d  = 1.8
b = (( d*a2*a2*c3*c3)/(32 *a3*a3*c2*c2)) *math.sqrt((- a3*c2)/( a1*c1))
c = (( a2*a2*c3*c3)/(4 *a3*c2)  - (a3*c1 + a1*c2)*b/d)/a2

def calculate (u, t, b, c):              # basic equation
    x, y, z = u
    # 3-layer
    dxdt = a1*x -a2*y + a3*z
    dydt = -d*x*z + b
    dzdt = c1*x*y + c2*y*z +c3*z + c
    return(dxdt, dydt, dzdt)

# start values and initialization
#y0 = 1.5, 1.5, 1.5     #y0 = -0.7, 0, 0
#y0 = 0.9, 0.9, 0.9     # y0 = 0.7, 0.7, 0.7
y0 = 0.5, 0.5, 0.5
t  = np.linspace (0, 10, 2000)
solution  = odeint(calculate , y0, t, args = (b, c))
X, Y, Z = solution [:,0],   solution [:,1],   solution [:,2]
```

XY

XZ

YZ

3d_3-layer

Zhou, T., Chen, G. (2004). A simple smooth chaotic system with a 3-layer attractor. International Journal of Bifurcation and Chaos, 14(05), 1795-1799, #83 3-Layer

```python
import numpy as np
import matplotlib.pyplot as plt
from mpl_toolkits.mplot3d import Axes3D
from scipy.integrate import odeint

# Parameter
picname = "Bouali_3"
a = 3.0
b = 2.2
c = 1.0
d = 0.001

# basic equation
def calculate (u, t, a, b):
    x, y, z = u
    # Bouali_3
    dxdt = a*x*(1-y) -b*z
    dydt = -c*y*(1-x*x)
    dzdt = d*x
    return(dxdt, dydt, dzdt)

# start values and initialization
y0 = 1, 0.1 , 0.1
#y0 = -1.0, 0.9, 1.0
t = np.linspace(0, 30, 3000)
solution = odeint(calculate , y0, t, args = (a, b))
X, Y, Z = solution [:,0], solution [:,1], solution [:,2]
```

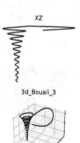

Bouali, S. (2013). A 3D strange attractor with a distinctive silhouette. The butterfly effect revisited, #84 Bouali3
url: https://shorturl.at/N5AXx

```
import math
import numpy as np
import matplotlib. pyplot as plt
from mpl_toolkits. mplot3d import Axes3D
from scipy.integrate import odeint

# Parameter
picname ="M01"
a = 1
b = 1

# basic equation
def calculate (u, t, a, b):
    x, y, z = u
    # M01
    dxdt = x*y - 60*y -75*z -x -x*z + y*y
    dydt = x*x + 65*x + y -(115/2) *z -y*z
    dzdt = y*y + (85/2) *y - 10*x -z
    return(dxdt, dydt, dzdt)

# start values and initialization
#y0 = 1.5, 1.5, 1.5      #y0 = 1.0, 1.0, 1.0
# y0 = 0.9, 0.9, 0.9     # y0 = 0.8, 0.8, 0.8
# y0 = 0.7, 0.7, 0.7     # y0 = 0.6, 0.6, 0.6
y0 = 0.5,  0.5,  0.5
t = np.linspace (0,  1,  5000)
solution  = odeint(calculate , y0, t, args = (a, b))
X, Y, Z = solution [:,0],   solution [:,1],   solution [:,2]
```

XY

XZ

YZ

3d_M01

Casas-García, K., Quezada-Téllez, L. A., Carrillo-Moreno, S., Flores-Godoy, J. J., Fernández-Anaya, G. (2016). Asymptotically stable equilibrium points in new chaotic systems. Nova scientia, 8(16), 41-58, #85 M01
url: https://shorturl.at/d7TrV

```python
import math
import numpy as np
import matplotlib. pyplot as plt
from mpl_toolkits. mplot3d import Axes3D
from scipy.integrate import odeint

# Parameter
picname ="M02"
a = 1
b = 1

# basic equation
def calculate (u, t, a, b):
    x, y, z = u
    # M02
    dxdt = 50*z -x - x*y -x*x
    dydt = -x*x -x*y -90*x -y*y + y*z -(175/2) *y + z*z
    dzdt = x*x -80*x -y*y + 20*z
    return(dxdt, dydt, dzdt)

# start values and initialization
#y0 = 1.5, 1.5, 1.5      #y0 = 1.0, 1.0, 1.0
# y0 = 0.9, 0.9, 0.9     # y0 = 0.8, 0.8, 0.8
# y0 = 0.7, 0.7, 0.7     # y0 = 0.6, 0.6, 0.6
y0 = 0.5, 0.5, 0.5
t = np.linspace (0, 1, 5000)
solution = odeint(calculate , y0, t, args = (a, b))
X, Y, Z = solution [:,0], solution [:,1], solution [:,2]
```

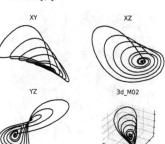

Casas-García, K., Quezada-Téllez, L. A., Carrillo-Moreno, S., Flores-Godoy, J. J., Fernández-Anaya, G. (2016). Asymptotically stable equilibrium points in new chaotic systems. Nova scientia, 8(16), 41-58, #86 M02
url: https://shorturl.at/d7TrV

```
import math
import numpy as np
import matplotlib.pyplot as plt
from mpl_toolkits.mplot3d import Axes3D
from scipy.integrate import odeint

# Parameter
picname ="M08"
a = 1
b = 1

# basic equation
def calculate (u, t, a, b):
    x, y, z = u
    # M08
    dxdt = x + (105/2) *y +z +y*z -y*y
    dydt = 40*x -y -(155/2) *z -x*z -x*x
    dzdt = y*y + 80*y + (135/2) *x -30*z
    return(dxdt, dydt, dzdt)

# start values and initialization
#y0 = 1.5, 1.5, 1.5      #y0 = 1.0, 1.0, 1.0
# y0 = 0.9, 0.9, 0.9     # y0 = 0.8, 0.8, 0.8
# y0 = 0.7, 0.7, 0.7     # y0 = 0.6, 0.6, 0.6
y0 = 0.5, 0.5, 0.5
t = np.linspace (0, 1, 5000)
solution = odeint(calculate , y0, t, args = (a, b))
X, Y, Z = solution [:,0], solution [:,1], solution [:,2]
```

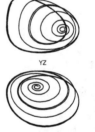

Casas-García, K., Quezada-Téllez, L. A., Carrillo-Moreno, S., Flores-Godoy, J. J., Fernández-Anaya, G. (2016). Asymptotically stable equilibrium points in new chaotic systems. Nova scientia, 8(16), 41-58, #87 M08
url: https://shorturl.at/d7TrV

```
import math
import numpy as np
import matplotlib. pyplot as plt
from mpl_toolkits. mplot3d import Axes3D
from scipy.integrate  import odeint

# Parameter
picname ="M09"
a = 1
b = 1

# basic equation
def calculate (u, t, a, b):
    x, y, z = u
    # M09
    dxdt = -(165/2) *x -70*y -z - y*z -y*y
    dydt = 55*z -(165/2) *x
    dzdt = y*z-80*y
    return(dxdt, dydt, dzdt)

# start values and initialization
#y0 = 1.5, 1.5, 1.5      #y0 = 1.0, 1.0, 1.0
# y0 = 0.9, 0.9, 0.9     # y0 = 0.8, 0.8, 0.8
# y0 = 0.7, 0.7, 0.7     # y0 = 0.6, 0.6, 0.6
y0 = 0.5,  0.5,  0.5
t  = np.linspace (0,  2,  10000)
solution  = odeint(calculate , y0, t, args = (a, b))
X, Y, Z = solution [:,0],  solution [:,1],   solution [:,2]
```

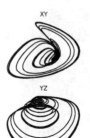

Casas-García, K., Quezada-Téllez, L. A., Carrillo-Moreno, S., Flores-Godoy, J. J., Fernández-Anaya, G. (2016). Asymptotically stable equilibrium points in new chaotic systems. Nova scientia, 8(16), 41-58, #88 M09
url: https://shorturl.at/d7TrV

```python
import math
import numpy as np
import matplotlib.pyplot as plt
from mpl_toolkits.mplot3d import Axes3D
from scipy.integrate import odeint

# Parameter
picname ="M10"
a = 1
b = 1

# basic equation
def calculate (u, t, a, b):
    x, y, z = u
    # M10
    dxdt = z-32.5*y-12.5*x-x*y+y*z+z*z
    dydt = -z
    dzdt = 47.5 *y-47.5*x+x*z-x*x+y*y
    return(dxdt, dydt, dzdt)

# start values and initialization
# y0 = 1.5, 1.5, 1.5     #y0 = 1.0, 1.0, 1.0
# y0 = 0.9, 0.9, 0.9     # y0 = 0.8, 0.8, 0.8
# y0 = 0.7, 0.7, 0.7     # y0 = 0.6, 0.6, 0.6
y0 = 0.5,  0.5,  0.5
t  = np.linspace (0,  3,  2000)
solution  = odeint(calculate , y0, t, args = (a, b))
X, Y, Z = solution [:,0],  solution [:,1],  solution [:,2]
```

Casas-García, K., Quezada-Téllez, L. A., Carrillo-Moreno, S., Flores-Godoy, J. J.,
Fernández-Anaya, G. (2016). Asymptotically stable equilibrium points in new chaotic
systems. Nova scientia, 8(16), 41-58, #89 M10
url: https://shorturl.at/d7TrV

```python
import math
import numpy as np
import matplotlib. pyplot  as  plt
from mpl_toolkits. mplot3d import Axes3D
from scipy.integrate   import odeint

picname ="HindmarshRose"              # Parameter
a = 0.49
b = 1
c = 0.0322
d = 1
s = 1
w = 0.03
v = 0.80

def calculate (u,  t,  a,  b):               # basic equation
    x,  y,  z = u
    # HindmarshRose
    dxdt = (-w*x +y -a*x*x*x + b*x*x +z)/w
    dydt = -a*x*x*x -(d-b)*x*x + z
    dzdt = (-s*x -z +c)/v
    return(dxdt,  dydt,  dzdt)

# start values and initialization
#y0 = 1.5, 1.5, 1.5  #y0 = 1.0, 1.0, 1.0  # y0 = 0.9, 0.9, 0.9
# y0 = 0.8, 0.8, 0.8 # y0 = 0.7, 0.7, 0.7 # y0 = 0.6, 0.6, 0.6
y0 = 0.5,  0.5,  0.5
t  = np.linspace (0,  30,  5000)
solution = odeint(calculate ,  y0, t,  args = (a, b))
X, Y,  Z = solution [:,0],    solution [:,1],    solution [:,2]
```

XY   XZ

YZ   3d_Hindmarsh-Rose

Hindmarsh J. L.; Rose R. M. (1984). "A model of neuronal bursting using three coupled first order differential equations". Proceedings of the Royal Society of London. Series B. Biological Sciences. 221 (1222): 87–102, #90 Hindmarsh-Rosen
url: https://doi.org/10.1098/rspb.1984.0024

Finally, we would like to point out once again that fractal computer graphics can be used to embellish not only walls in rooms. Postcard-sized graphics can also attract attention and demand for different occasions. This can be done in different ways with *matplotlib*. A simple example could look like this:

```python
import numpy as np
import matplotlib.pyplot as plt
from mpl_toolkits.mplot3d import Axes3D
from scipy.integrate import odeint

# Parameter
picname = "Sakarya"
a = 0.4
b = 0.3

# basic equation
def calculate (u, t, a, b):
    x, y, z = u
    # Sakarya
    dxdt = -x+y+(y*z)
    dydt = -x-y+a*(x*z)
    dzdt = z-b*(x*y)
    return(dxdt, dydt, dzdt)

# start values and initialization
y0 = 1, -1, 1
t = np.linspace (0, 40, 2000)
#t = np.linspace(0, 70, 4000)
solution = odeint(calculate , y0, t, args = (a, b))
X, Y, Z = solution [:,0], solution [:,1], solution [:,2]

fig_b = plt.figure ()

################# start of create the birthday box
plt.rc('font', size =12)
plt.axis("Off")
plt.text (0.5, 0.55, "Happy Birthday", size =50, rotation =30.,
        ha="center", va="center",
        bbox=dict(boxstyle ="round",
                  ec=(1., 0.5, 0.5),
                  fc =(1., 0.8, 0.8),
                  )
        )
################# end of create the birthday box

ax_b = fig_b.add_subplot(111, title ="Ada Lovelace, 10. Dezember")
ax_b.axis ("Off")
ax_b.plot (X, Z, "black")
fig_b.savefig (picname + "_XZ.pdf", bbox_inches='tight') # Save a .pdf file
#fig_b.savefig(picname + "_XZ.png", bbox_inches='tight')  # Save a .png file
plt.show()
```

Ada Lovelace, 10. Dezember

As you can easily see, only a small code fragment has been added next to a heading (Ada Lovelace[1], 10 December), which contains a larger text (Happy Birthday) tilted at an angle. However, if one wants to create other or more complex images with information texts, one should look more intensively into the possibilities of the graphic library.

A long time has passed since the beginnings of chaos theory and the discovery of fractal structures. Many of the fractals presented here, which can be described by differential equations, first saw the light of day in scientific papers at that time. For those interested in these articles, we have found some through internet research. They are listed in the code archive. In the citation list of the articles, you will find additional code numbers of the type #000 next to the year. These numbers refer to the images numbered in the same way in the book. Even a fractal cookbook often provides only a limited number of recipes. However, the number of possible fractal dishes is greater because with the variation of ingredients, parameters, more cooking results can be realized than existing recipes.

Here we give again the complete recipe for the cooking process. The procedure is always the same. Only ingredient number 1 has to be changed in each case.

---

[1]   The birthday wish noted here is for Ada Lovelace, who worked with Charles Babbage on the first computer, the *Analytical Engine*. Ada recognized the potential of the first mechanical computer and may have been the world's first female programmer.

Lorenz Appetizer *Lorenz graphic in paper coat*

For 1 person, duration 15 min

Craft: easy Ingredients: QR code amount part 1 (Lorenz), QR code amount part 2 (basic food graphic).

- QR-code part 1 Scan and send by email (or otherwise) to destination address,
- QR code part 2 Scan and send by email (or other means) to destination address.
- Start IDE Thonny and insert the copied part 1 and part 2 in the editor.
- Check and create the Python indentation structure in the Thonny editor.
- Start (compile) correct Python Thonny code.
- Send generated graphic to printer and be happy ....

We have already mentioned several times that images can also be created without the headings above the computer graphics. For computer graphics without a heading the corresponding *subplot* command in the main program must be changed. We therefore present an example here (Thomas-Attraktor, #63)[2] WITHOUT the headings available.

Part 1 (calculate) | Part 2 (main) without headings

---

2 QR code: left side part 1, right side part 2
   Part 1 of the central code is replaced in each case
   Part 2 of the central code remains unchanged in each case

The last example still contains all variants of images. If you only want to produce a single image, the main program is shortened to a few lines. The parameters for the desired coordinates (xy, yz, xz, zy etc.) must of course be adapted. Please study the shortened example of the Thomas attractor required for this:

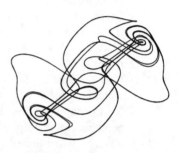

Thomas attractor Z,Y QR code | computer graphics fractal duck (?)

```
1  import numpy as np
2  import matplotlib. pyplot as plt
3  from mpl_toolkits. mplot3d import Axes3D
4  from scipy.integrate  import odeint
```

Lines 1 to 4 only contain the calls for the central libraries.

Lines 2 to 22 contain the central calculate method for the Thomas attractor.

```
5   # Parameter
6   picname ="Thomas"
7   a = 1
8   b = 0.19
9   # basic equation
10  def calculate (u, t, a, b):
11      x, y, z = u
12      # Thomas
13      dxdt = -b*x + np.sin(y)
14      dydt = -b*y + np.sin(z)
15      dzdt = -b*z + np.sin(x)
16      return(dxdt, dydt, dzdt)

18  # start values and initialization
19  y0 = -1.0, 0.9, 1.0
20  t = np.linspace(0, 340, 2000)
21  solution = odeint(calculate, y0, t, args = (a, b))
22  X, Y, Z = solution[:,0], solution[:,1], solution[:,2]
```

Lines 24 to 33 contain the central main program with adjustments for the coordinate display Z,Y.
The computer graphic is saved as a ThomasZY.png, ThomasZY.pdf, ThomasZY.svg document.

```
24  ########################### short main (!)
25  fig_a =plt.figure ()
26  #no Title
27  ax_a= fig_a.add_subplot(111, title ="")
28  ax_a.axis ("Off")
29  ax_a.plot (Z, Y, "black")        #select parameters of ↩
            the coordinates
30  fig_a.savefig (picname + "_ZY.pdf", bbox_inches='tight ')
31  fig_a.savefig (picname + "_ZY.png", bbox_inches='tight ')
32  fig_a.savefig (picname + "_ZY.svg", bbox_inches='tight ')
33  plt.show()
```

Have fun experimenting! Bon appetit! Last but not least, here are a few more examples ...

 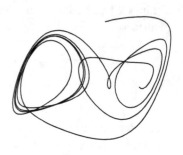

#11 ChuaCubic X,Y QR Code | Computer Graphics

 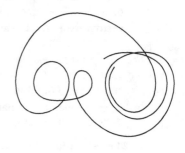

#12 Coulett X,Y QR Code | Computer Graphics

#17 FourWing2 X,Y Code | Computer Graphics

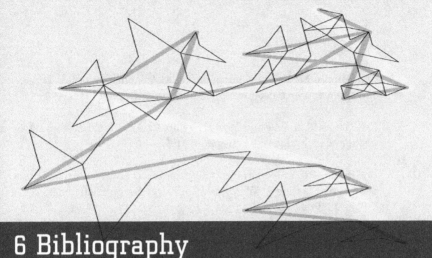

6 Bibliography

[01] William M. Newman, W. N. Newman, and Robert F. Sproull. Principles of Interactive Computer Graphics -. New York: McGraw- Hill, 1979. ISBN: 978-0-070-46338-7.

[02] Harold Abelson and Andrea Disessa. Turtle Geometry - The Computer as a Medium for Exploring Mathematics. Cambridge: MIT Press, 1986. ISBN: 978-0-262-51037-0. doi: 10 . 1155 / S1026022698000041 .

[03] Michael F Barnsley et al. The science of fractal images. Vol. 1. Springer, 1988.

[04] Karl-Heinz Becker and Michael Dörfler. Dynamical Systems and Fractals - Computer Graphics Experiments with Pascal. Cambridge: Cambridge University Press, 1989. ISBN: 978-0-521-36910-7.

[05] John Briggs. Fractals: The patterns of chaos: A new aesthetic of art, science, and nature. Simon and Schuster, 1992.

[06] Heinz-Otto Peitgen, Hartmut Jürgens, and Dietmar Saupe. Chaos - Bausteine der Ordnung. Berlin, Heidelberg: Springer, 1994. ISBN: 978-3-608-95435-7.

[07] Alfredo Medio and Giampaolo Gallo. Chaotic dynamics: Theory and applications to economics. Cambridge University Press, 1995.

[08] Gregory L Baker and Jerry P Gollub. Chaotic dynamics: an introduction. Cambridge university press, 1996.

[09] Heinz-Otto Peitgen, Hartmut Jürgens, and Dietmar Saupe. Bausteine des Chaos Fraktale -. Wiesbaden: Springer Berlin Heidelberg, 2012. ISBN: 978-3-642-93525-1.

[10] Armin Bunde and Shlomo Havlin. Fractals in science. Springer, 2013.

[11] Karl-Heinz Becker and Michael Dörfler. Dynamische Systeme und Fraktale - Computergrafische Experimente mit Pascal. Berlin Heidelberg New York: Springer-Verlag, 2013. ISBN: 978-3-663-00168-3.

[12] B. Mandelbrot. Die fraktale Geometrie der Natur -. Berlin Heidelberg New York: Springer-Verlag, 2013. ISBN: 978-3-034-85027-8.

[13] Michael F Barnsley. Fractals everywhere. Academic press, 2014.

[14] Heinz-Otto Peitgen and Peter H. Richter. The Beauty of Fractals -. Berlin, Heidelberg: Springer, 2014. ISBN: 978-3-642-61718-8.

[15] John Argyris et al. Die Erforschung des Chaos - Dynamische Systeme. Berlin Heidelberg New York: Springer-Verlag, 2017. ISBN: 978-3-662-54546-1.

[16] Jeffrey Ventrella. The Family Tree of Fractal Curves -. Eyebrain Books, 2019. ISBN: 978-0-983-05463-4.

[17] Benoit Mandelbrot. Fractals - Form, Chance, and Dimension. Brattleboro: Echo Point Books and Media,Reprint ed. Edition, 2020. ISBN: 978-1635618549.

[18] International Journal of Bifurcation and Chaos in Applied Sciences and Engineering ISSN (print): 0218-1274 | ISSN (online): 1793-6551

> For those who enjoy the interesting computer graphics, we would like to add a note.
> There is a book series on *Chaostheory and Fractals* whose programmes are formulated using the software development environment *Processing*. In Processing you can write programs in Java syntax and/or Python syntax. We call the two Processing versions *ProcessingJava* and *ProcessingPython* respectively, depending on the type.

- **Volume 1: Fractals and Dynamical Systems**
  This book introduces the basics of chaos theory and dynamic systems and encourages with many examples to computer-graphic experiments with the programming language Processing. There is an extra volume for book 1 (*Code Archive - Fractals and Dynamic Systems*), which contains the programs as source code and QR code.
- **Volume 2: Fractals XXL - Picture Book of Fractals**
  This book deals with a special form of fractals, also called *strange attractors*. In particular, two forms are examined, which we call *DynFractals* and *GeoFractals*.
  DynFractals are based on systems of differential equations that can be modelled by iteration equations.
  GeoFractals are self-similar structures that can be generated by recursion equations in a coordinate system grid.
- **Volume 3: Newton Fractals**
  This book deals with a special variant of complex polynomial equations, the Newton fractals, which can produce particularly beautiful and colourful computer graphics. The computer graphics are formulated using the Python programming language.

The mathematical principles are explained in all 3 volumes. The prerequisites for understanding are elementary and do not require any in-depth mathematical knowledge. All volumes contain the computer programs used to generate the images.

The book *Cooking Recipes for Fractals* deals with the topic of dynamic fractals in a different, alternative way by using only the programming language Python and the mathematical *odeint* function to formulate the algorithms for graphical visualization. It does not contain any mathematical explanations, as it is only a collection of recipes.

Index

www.ingramcontent.com/pod-product-compliance
Lightning Source LLC
LaVergne TN
LVHW051343050326
832903LV00031B/3715